THE EMERGENCY

THE EMERGENCY

A Year of Healing and Heartbreak in a Chicago ER

THOMAS FISHER

ONE WORLD

NEW YORK

The Emergency is a work of nonfiction. The stories told in this book are based upon or derived from real-world medical situations. Most names and identifying details have been changed. With few exceptions, characters (both patients and hospital personnel) are edited composites of real people. The timing of when these medical experiences happened in relation to one another has also been changed. Resemblance to persons living or dead resulting from these changes is entirely coincidental and unintentional. While the events discussed in this book took place at the University of Chicago's Emergency Department, the events described can and do occur at other medical centers, clinics, and hospitals.

Published in the United States by One World, an imprint of Random House, a division of Penguin Random House LLC, New York.

ONE WORLD and colophon are registered trademarks of Penguin Random House LLC.

Library of Congress Cataloging-in-Publication Data

Names: Fisher, Thomas, author.
Title: The emergency: a year of healing and heartbreak in a
Chicago ER / by Thomas Fisher.
Description: First edition. | New York: One World, [2022] | Includes index.
Identifiers: LCCN 2021039073 (print) | LCCN 2021039074 (ebook) |
ISBN 9780593230671 (hardcover) | ISBN 9780593230688 (ebook)
Subjects: LCSH: African Americans—Medical care. |
African Americans—Health and hygiene. | Minorities—Medical care. |
Medical care—Social aspects. | Discrimination in medical care. |
Equality—Health aspects. | Hospitals—Emergency services.
Classification: LCC RA448.5.N4 F57 2022 (print) | LCC RA448.5.N4 (ebook) |
DDC 362.1089/96073—dc23

LC record available at lccn.loc.gov/2021039073
LC ebook record available at lccn.loc.gov/2021039074

Printed in the United States of America on acid-free paper

oneworldlit.com
randomhousebooks.com

1st Printing

First Edition

Designed by Debbie Glasserman

FOR MY PATIENTS,
WHOSE PERSEVERANCE, BEAUTY, AND GRACE
REMIND ME OF WHAT MATTERS

It should not be doubted that human life could be prolonged,
if we knew the appropriate art.

RENÉ DESCARTES, *DISCOURSE ON METHOD* (1637)

CONTENTS

FOREWORD

Ta-Nehisi Coates

ONE EVENING IN 2005, I drove over to see an old friend and classmate in the Bronzeville section of Chicago. Natalie Moore—
"Big Nat," as we called her—had attended Howard with me and
worked on the school newspaper. As young journalists, we had
probably planned an evening of catching up and comparing
craft notes. But there wasn't much craft discussed that evening,
if only to keep from boring Big Nat's other guest: Thomas
"Tom" Fisher. Tom and Nat had both grown up on the South
Side and had been friends since childhood. I'd met Tom at Howard, where he would occasionally visit Nat. Beyond a love of
food, drink, and crude jokes, what the three of us shared was a
deep sense that our work must serve our community. For Nat
and me, that responsibility manifested itself in our approach to
journalism—the stories we told, the people we highlighted, the
arguments we advanced. But for Tom, who'd just finished his

residency in emergency medicine, that responsibility was always more direct.

I remember how we commiserated over takeout and libations. I remember the "oh my people" jokes we made as music videos scrolled across the screen. But more than anything that happened in that apartment that night, I remember what happened outside it. When I'd first arrived hours earlier, I'd seen a group of young brothers seated on the stoop across from Nat's apartment. They were having a party of their own. I pulled up, got out of my car, nodded the silent greeting of Black people the world over, and kept it moving. A few hours later, we heard gunshots. There was almost no alarm among us, save for the collective note that the shots seemed rather close. But we kept the party going until we saw police lights strobing through the windows. It was time to leave anyway. When Tom and I stepped outside, what we saw in the streets of Bronzeville was no great shock to either of us—police tape on the sidewalk, the body of a young Black man laid out on the concrete—but the moment is still indelible for me. And whatever weight it put on me, I knew even then, did not compare to what Tom would have to carry.

It was not merely that Tom was an ER doctor directly caring for those affected by the plague of gun violence that covered the country and levied a particular toll on Black neighborhoods. It was that those bodies were rushed into the ER from the streets that Tom called home. He was working not just for the Black community in general but for the same South Side of Chicago where his parents had settled and where he had been raised; he was caring for the lives and bodies of his neighbors. I don't think it's too much to say that the lion's share of Tom's professional life has been consumed not only by treating the kind of violence we bore witness to that evening, but by an urgent attempt to understand why that violence tends to fall with such weight on the South Sides of America while barely grazing its Gold Coasts. It is those two labors that fill the pages of *The Emergency:* the work of Dr. Fisher's hands, treating patients in the midst of a pandemic, and the work of his mind, trying to understand the larger system that delivers so many broken bodies from these streets into his care.

The answers he arrives at are not comforting. African Americans rank at the bottom of virtually every socioeconomic indicator. Health care is no exception. Explanations for this tend to focus on individual behavior. Confronted with the shocking death rates befalling Black people in the wake of COVID-19, Surgeon General Jerome Adams asserted that the Black community needed to "step up" and "avoid alcohol, tobacco and drugs." "Do it for your Big Momma," Adams asserted. "Do it for your Pop-Pop." There is no data that shows Black people drinking, smoking, or drugging more than anyone else (and some that indicates they do so less.) But the point is comfort, not data. And it is simply more comforting to believe that the disproportionate impact of the worst pandemic in American history could have been avoided if Black people were monastic.

But *The Emergency* joins a disturbing consensus increasingly being reached in the scholarship of power—the vast chasms between the haves and have-nots of America are rarely benign mistakes amenable to behavioralism. The work of Ira Katznelson, Beryl Satter, and Richard Rothstein has demonstrated that the yawning wealth gap is the result not of poor spending habits but of federal policy. Eve Ewing's research into Chicago's schools shows how "school reform" in Black communities ultimately destroyed the last outposts of the state, short of law enforcement. Devah Pager's studies of employment and incarceration show that employers evaluated Black men with no criminal record the same as white men *with* a criminal record. Moreover, this scholarship has demonstrated that the relationship between the powerful and the powerless is parasitic. The historian Edmund Morgan does not merely condemn American slavery but demonstrates how American notions of freedom depended upon it.

This is the tradition out of which *The Emergency* emerges. What it shows is that the health-care chasm is not an accident but a feature of white supremacy and American capitalism. But unlike the journalists, sociologists, and historians who must painstakingly recreate events and power dynamics from archives and interviews, Tom is a direct observer. He has seen the machine from every possible vantage—as a doctor operating within it, as a public health scholar studying it, as a White House fellow working to shape policy, and as health-care leader trying to implement that policy. He comes to understand that long wait times in ERs like his on the South Side cost lives and allow for the spread of misery; that those wait times differ drastically from those in hospitals mere miles away; that the misery in one ER and the satisfaction in another are linked. He shows how even within a hospital ostensibly serving a poorer and blacker clientele, the relentless laws of capitalism lead the hospital to consider erecting a system of de facto Jim Crow health care.

To demonstrate this, Tom unearths a factor that those in power seek so often to obscure: the state. It is a trick of members of the corporate class and their followers to depict their success as the correct outcome of a working market. But *The Emergency* shows how that enterprise is subsidized by the state—

doctor training funded by the public, research underwritten by government grants, patients insured by government programs. And despite the public subsidization of health care, the public benefits vary according to class. The residents of the South Side that Tom cares for are ostensible participants in the American social contract—its edicts and its bounty. But the former land harder on them than the latter. And despite being a part of the public that subsidizes health care, they do not get their fair share of the returns.

The Emergency renders the impact of this capricious system in visceral detail. Pain and agony are everywhere, but a look at the system through a doctor's eyes reveals that Black people do not merely live shorter lives than their peers; their lives are more physically agonizing. And this is not just the agony of illness and injury, but the compounding of that illness and injury by the sheer fact of racism. "Your body, like many bodies on the South Side, began accumulating injury and illness before the bodies of your peers on the North Side," Tom writes to a patient. "And unlike your peers, you had fewer chances to recover and return to your prior health."

Through it all, the author moves like a blur, going from patient to patient doing his best to heal the body, "our most important endowment." He almost always comes up short. And that is because even as a doctor, he is merely an actor within the system, not its author. And at the climax of *The Emergency*, the system reaches out to touch not just Tom's neighbors but his family.

The Emergency is not just a year in the life of an ER during COVID but a powerful examination of the entire complex of health care and the inequalities that bend it. It is worth remembering the early days of COVID's arrival, when it was said to be "colorblind." Maybe we wanted to believe that in a true crisis we would find ourselves together, on even footing, if only in our common human frailty. But now here we are, two years later, with Blacks and Latinos having lost some three years of life expectancy over the course of the pandemic—triple that of whites. We should have known better. *We should now know better.*

The Emergency explains why, be it the plague of gun violence or the plague of COVID, the burden is never borne equally.

THE EMERGENCY

I

FEBRUARY 2020

WE HAD BEEN WAITING for the virus to appear in our ER, but when it did, a heavy pall still fell on the department. Unmasked nurses with long faces spoke in hushed voices and laughed nervously as the patient was directed to Room 41, a negative pressure room that had been designed in 2015 to contain Ebola. The negative pressure in the room keeps the patient's air from contaminating the rest of the department, and the room has a window and microphone in the wall so that we can communicate with the patient while remaining safe outside. Before I entered the antechamber between the common ER hall and the room, I put on a yellow gown, an N95 mask shaped like a duckbill, and a disposable plastic eye shield that I placed over my glasses. The nurse, Fred, was similarly protected, and together we leapt from the safety of the boat into the dark abyss.

I first met the leviathan on New Year's Eve less than two

months earlier. "China investigates outbreak of atypical pneumonia that is suspected linked to SARS," tweeted Agence
France-Presse on the morning of December 31, 2019. At the
time, I had been following foreign media for human signs of the
flu that was culling a third of Asia's hogs. But this was not swine
flu. Rapidly spreading and deadly infections threaten everyone
who works in emergency rooms. We fear the day that a pan-
icked traveler shows up with a high fever and an unusual rash. In
the time it takes to figure out what's going on, the patient would
be able to infect all the nurses and doctors who try to help. That
nightmare kept me vigilant for deadly viruses and outbreaks of
hemorrhagic fevers no matter where they are on the globe, but
so far, I had only experienced misses.

In 2001, when anthrax spores were mailed to politicians and
journalists, our waiting room filled with healthy patients worried that they had been exposed to a "white powder." Thirteen
years later Ebola swept the world, and I drilled donning and
doffing head-to-toe protective equipment for the seemingly inevitable febrile patient bleeding from eyes and nose. Now, as this
unusual pneumonia bloomed into tens then hundreds of cases,
my curiosity turned into something else: fear. When *The New
York Times* took note in a January 8, 2020, article nestled deep
within the global health section, I forwarded the item to friends
along with a caveat: "This may not be a looming pandemic, but
when the next one occurs, this is how it will start."

All of January and most of February elapsed before the first
symptomatic patient arrived on the South Side, where I worked
as an emergency room doctor at the University of Chicago. By
then the coronavirus had been dubbed COVID-19 and had in-

fected people on every continent. At last, in late February, a febrile traveler named Terri came to us with a cough and a story.
A flight attendant had coughed in her face on her way to Seattle,
a city already besieged by the virus. As Seattle's ICUs swelled
with infected people, Terri, a middle-aged businesswoman,
shook hands in meetings and dined with clients. On the flight
back she broke into a fever and developed a hacking cough.
After googling "best hospital in Chicago," she grabbed a cab
from Midway and came directly to our Emergency Department.

Terri coughed behind her blue surgical mask but greeted
Fred and me in good spirits. Dwarfed by the proportions of
Room 41, a room designed to accommodate a dialysis machine
and a ventilator, she lay semi-reclined, red-faced and sweaty on
the gurney. As she was complaining of body aches and nausea, I
made a call to the hospital epidemiologist and ordered tests for
the virus, a chest CT, and an admission to the hospital to keep
her isolated until we confirmed her illness.

Terri's vital signs remained stable despite a fever that Tylenol
did not break. I could hear her cough through the closed double
doors on her room—each time, my shoulders tensed. We tested
our infection precautions every year, but even so, Fred forgot to
take off his protective wear when he returned to the ER from
the murky depths of Room 41. While he was sending blood to
the lab for tests, Fred left the isolation room door open, setting
off a squealing alarm. Sweating and nervous, he apologized repeatedly for these miscues. I told him that it was okay, but we
both knew these social graces were meaningless. The virus
doesn't care about our apologies or forgiveness. Diagnosing and
treating an illness we'd never seen before while keeping our

lungs and mucous membranes safe was going to require vigilance and stamina.

A week later, Americans awoke to a society unraveling in the wake of the monster's cross-country frenzy. As the infection spread, businesses reduced hours, then closed altogether and laid off workers. On March 9 the stock market crashed. Deaths mounted from one to tens to a hundred. I canceled my boys' trip to Vegas for March Madness. Our country's retreat progressed from there. An NBA player tested positive; the NBA abandoned its season; then all sports seasons were terminated. Chicago Public Schools had fought to extend its year after a fall strike, but it soon sent kids home indefinitely. Drunk young people, slurring their speech and draped over one another, spread the infection over St. Patrick's Day and pushed our governor to close bars and restaurants and prohibit all nonessential travel. By then the virus's campaign had gripped the world's economy, culture, and routines. Seattle nursing homes had been wiped clean; in Italy refrigerator trucks filled with bodies; my colleagues in New York were exhausted—and infected.

Friends across the country reached out for my advice on when to take their kids out of school or whether to take their planned vacation to Jamaica. I couldn't make those decisions, but I did share my understanding of the situation and its risks. I directly addressed the misinformation emanating from Facebook and the White House—I told them that this would *not* quickly disappear and that it was *not* a hoax. Each time my friends asked how many people would die, I considered withholding information from the models that forecast millions of dead Americans. While that would have been soothing, obscuring key information from those I care about undermines lifesaving decisions. Offering that the equivalent of Denver could die in a matter of months stuck in my throat. Sometimes we had to end the call.

Then the plague closed in on me from another direction. On March 23 my uncle fell ill, and three days later he was admitted to the intensive care unit. Uncle Robert was the one who took me to Tigers baseball games and rode bikes with me when I was a kid. In retirement from teaching in the Detroit Public Schools, he developed a chronic illness and landed in a care facility that didn't protect him. As with millions of other Americans who'd been warehoused or discarded—seniors, prisoners, migrant workers in airless camps, people who society preferred to keep out of sight—the virus fell on his body hard. Uncle Robert was lucky; after a few days of gasping in the ICU, he recovered. And then it came for the South Side.

COVID smashed through the South Side's multigenerational homes. This is a neighborhood packed with people who don't have the sort of white-collar jobs that let you work from home—with nothing but a frayed safety net to hold them if they fell, they had to risk their bodies just to keep from starving. And when they came home, they exposed the vulnerable elders who often lived with them. The devastation was a literal manifestation of the old truism "When America catches a cold, Black America gets pneumonia."

Even back in January, I knew that the onslaught was inevitable. No matter how I prepared, I expected to be infected before it was over. Scores of physicians around the world had already died. As their lungs became stiff and wet, they were attended by peers rendered unrecognizable by protective garments. Li Wen-liang, the thirty-four-year-old Wuhan doctor who alerted the world to the monster, was one of the first to die. A man about my age, facing down the pandemic just as I was going to, was lost in its wake. When I read about Li's death, it strangely brought me back to 1999 and the killing of Robert Russ. I hadn't thought about the story in years. Russ was around my age and was just about to graduate from Northwestern when a Chicago police officer shot him dead in a police stop. I didn't know Russ; I'd only read about him in the newspaper, just as I was now reading about Li. But there were similarities in our lives that had chilled me as I read his story: at the time we were both college-age Black men who faced traffic stops from the same police department. Both Russ and Li were innocent, both lost to a lethal scourge that strikes down victims who share a portion of their identity. Just as in 1999, I now searched for the balance between fear of death, anger at the unfairness, and comfort in the long odds.

The only question I had was: how sick will I become? The only certainty is that once I'm infected, I will be contagious, and I can't risk passing the disease along to my family, my patients, or the woman I think I love. So the terrifying months ahead will be spent mostly alone. It feels cruel that I will be without human touch during the most stressful time of my life, but the alternative is to infect the people who mean the most to me.

As stores were emptied of toilet paper and shuttered in late March, our family group text buzzed with plans. I let my family know at my niece's muted first-birthday celebration that I wouldn't see them for a while, to protect them from infection. With primary-colored helium balloons floating to the ceiling, my announcement turned it into a going-away party. Later, a physician group chat churned with anxious messages about securing better protective equipment. Hospital preparations included a schedule for doctors to cover for those who fell ill and alternative housing for folks who couldn't go home. I prepared my affairs—set up autopay for my mortgage, stocked my freezer, and withdrew cash as though I'd be gone for six months. My will was up-to-date.

2

MARCH 2020

I PREPARE FOR MY shift with gospel music. I'm a nonpracticing agnostic, but today the gospel themes of hope, sacrifice, and community give me comfort. The music is expressive, a release, an offering, a plea. Hope birthed by Black folks during our darkest days. My skin runs with goosebumps from a choir in full swing while I gather an extra N95, clean my eye protection, and find my ID for my first evening working in the hot zone. I feel an odd cycling of impulses—swollen with courage, knowing I've prepared for this my whole life. Ready to sprint away.

Doctors are accustomed to the possibility of looming death when we go to work—but usually not our own. It is strange that we are sometimes seen as heroic for doing our jobs, when it's the patient whose life is on the line. Of the invisible markers that set me apart from my patients—sometimes class, sometimes education, sometimes race, sometimes sex, sometimes age, sometimes power—the clearest marker is that one of us is

sick and one of us is not. But this virus muddies that distinction—
its transmissibility means the line between us might collapse,
the work of healing suddenly laced with the threat of sickness,
maybe even death. This new threat does not change my obliga-
tion or oath. If I meet my end caring for people, I tell myself
over and over again, then this is an acceptable way to go.

But my subconscious is not as confident. Last night I woke
up at 2 A.M., tachycardic, tense, and wondering whether I'm
going to walk into an emergency department full of sick and
dying patients. Sleep brought nightmares of having to decide
who lives and dies based on limited time and scarce materials. In
those dreams I was judge and executioner rather than caregiver.
I tossed with panic that my parents would fall ill and that I
wouldn't be able to help before they died all alone. Nevertheless, at 6:30 my alarm sounds, the sun rises, and I make coffee.

The virus changes everything. What to wear, how to get to
the hospital, when to eat, and every step of patient care has
to be rethought in order to stay safe. I borrow my parents' car to
get myself to work, now that ride shares are too risky. Normally
I choose which of my own scrubs to wear to work, but today
there's no need to linger over that decision, because I'll change
into blue hospital-supplied scrubs when I arrive and change
back when I'm done to reduce the amount of virus I transport.
After showering and dressing, I pack water and snacks to devour
on the twenty-minute ride back home, as I don't plan to remove
my mask to eat or drink over my eight-hour shift. Once home,
I'll undress in the hallway outside my apartment, come in
naked, drop my hospital scrubs in the washing machine, and
shower. I hope that my neighbors Joseph and Dianne don't
catch a glimpse of my striptease, but neighbors rarely linger

outside their apartments anymore. Before I leave, I place a clean towel in the bathroom and leave the door open so I won't have to touch the handle on my way to the shower. A friend who saw combat in the Middle East reassures me that once I'm in the ER I'll feel comfortable and my training will allow me to focus on the situation. For now, everything seems new and difficult.

It's an overcast day with sharp gusts of Chicago wind. Heading south, the roads are remarkably full—we are about a month into lockdown, and I'm expecting the roads to be clear. But the drivers are numerous and aggressive, as if this is just a typical rush hour. I turn to WBMX 104.3 FM, the old-school hip-hop station, and nod to "Bonita Applebum." The traffic clears. Darting down the Dan Ryan Expressway past empty train platforms and the vacant stadium, I rev the engine, thrilled by acceleration. Exiting at Garfield Boulevard, I pull to the intersection. There I'm greeted by a spotless gold 1992 Coupe de Ville with chrome hammers, and by ramp workers panhandling. A man in a wheelchair with an amputated leg pushes himself across the street, and another, short in stature with a grizzled beard, sells socks down the block. As I make my way through the South Side streets, I realize there are no women out, only Black men, and no one is stopping to engage with anyone else. I proceed down Garfield through deserted Washington Park, whose grass is starting to turn green. Soon the budding trees will be encircled by purple flowers making fairy rings in the same grass where many of our trauma patients fall bleeding. The hospital sign, THE UNIVERSITY OF CHICAGO MEDICINE, looms just over the park's bare trees, and I arrive at the hospital thirty minutes early. I park the car on the street near the Emergency Department entrance and don my protective eyewear and a mask before walking in. My goggles fog up with each breath.

The ER is empty. Security guards greet me with a nod and "Where you been, Doc?"—they're unrecognizable in their procedure masks and eyewear. The only other person in the waiting area is the nurse who checks everyone's temperature before they enter. Silence has replaced the usual cacophony of coughs, moans, and talking. Empty chairs and blaring TVs make the waiting room seem hastily evacuated just before my arrival. The area where patients usually wait hunched in wheelchairs is unoccupied, and the plastic seats designed for ease of cleaning rather than comfort are vacant. I swipe my ID to enter the treatment area, turn right and up through the private passageway to the scrub machine, where I pick up large-size scrubs and head to the locker room. Normally I arrive two minutes before my shift, throw things in my locker, and get right to work, but today requires a more methodical transition. I close the bathroom door behind me and am taking off my personal scrubs to change into the crisp hospital scrubs when I realize there's nowhere to put my clothes. The coed locker room does not have the privacy to change clothes and the sparse bathroom has no ledges or counters; all that's left is the dirty floor. I'll need a new plan.

My shift is in a section newly built for the pandemic, reclaimed from the parking garage. The smell of fresh drywall and paint seep through my mask. Parking spaces have been transformed into a waiting room and treatment area for people with flu-like symptoms. To enter I have to climb stairs and then pass a new sign warning, BEYOND THIS POINT PROTECTIVE EQUIPMENT IS REQUIRED. Our makeshift hot zone. My hair is

covered, eyes behind goggles and face shielded by a mask. My
heart races but everyone else seems calm, like this is a normal
day. Two nurses concealed head to toe with personal protective
equipment (PPE) greet me with joyful voices. "Hey, Dr. Fisher!"
The PPE masks their identity—how do they know it's me? I try
to match their energy with my own "Hey, y'all." The area is
packed with patients, each in a stacking chair exactly six feet
apart. People are bundled up, sniffling and coughing. These are
not monsters; no one sprouted horns and grew hooves once infected with COVID-19. These are the same Black folks as before,
up against yet another hazard trying to kill them.

My patients are South Siders, Black folks whose grandparents
fled terrorism in the American South to jobs in Chicago. This
community shaped Mahalia Jackson's voice, guided the surgical
precision of Daniel Hale Williams, and molded Barack Obama
into presidential form. My patients' labor, organizing, and crea-
tivity built this country. Their suffering, exploitation, and deaths
are also woven into the fabric of America. These communities
have been devalued by segregation and are often designated
"crime-ridden" or "food deserts." Efforts to address these conditions are too often frustrated by Chicago's notorious political
"machine," which distributes buildings and benefits according
to loyalty, patronage, and hierarchy. Still laboring in public while
white-collar workers sit at home, they queue up coughing and
febrile. As I feared, the virus has sickened scores.

As the attending physician I supervise the care of each patient in the Emergency Department. Like attending physicians
in EDs across the country, I don't get involved with every decision, but I meet and examine each patient and I am ultimately
responsible for their diagnosis, treatment plan, and outcome.

The residents are the ones who put their hands on every patient. We discuss every case, then they run resuscitations and prescribe medications with my support and feedback. With each level of training, residents gain more and more autonomy. Their documents and orders direct the nurses and techs, who draw blood, deliver medications, perform EKGs, and measure vital signs. The nurses and techs spend more time with patients than any doctor does. If anyone on the team is off their game, the whole choreography falls apart. But when the dance is flowing as it should, it takes on a kind of frantic beauty.

Less than an hour into my shift we get notice that a shooting with multiple victims is sending three people our way. When I hear the trauma code, I leave the hot zone and hustle back through the ED, put on a blue plastic gown and swipe my ID to open the locked doors to the ambulance bay. I arrive just in time to see the first victim roll out of Ambulance 38 on a gurney. I look through my protective goggles at a young man with full, long dreads. His eyes are partially open and unfocused. His head lolls to the side as a paramedic holding a finger to the young man's neck shouts "He's lost a pulse!" I am on the periphery of the scene, this is not my patient, but I watch intently in case I'm needed. The paramedics, gurney, and the ten-person trauma team run toward Room 41 to resuscitate him. There is an airway team waiting for him, so I stand out of the way as surgeons, nurses, and techs hurry in and out with surgical trays, packs of blood, and tools to desperately try to revive the young man.

Back in the doorway of the ambulance bay, the next patient is mine. A woman who says she's in her thirties but looks like she's in her fifties is bleeding from her leg. She's stable, so I usher her into the trauma room for a full evaluation. With smoker's lips and hair loss from braided styles that have pulled her hair out on the sides, she sits there with bloody jeans and a gunshot wound in her left shin. The leg is bent at an awkward angle, but when I touch it, it's warm and has a pulse. Before we have her fully evaluated, we are called over to an older gentleman in his sixties being rolled into the trauma bay, fresh from an ambulance. He was crossing the street when he was hit by a car. A Black man in baggy jeans and a workman's flannel shirt under a puffy coat, he's swearing in Spanish and trying to describe the pain he's in. The nurse translates—or at least translates some of it: the pain is in his hip. Since the resuscitation in Room 41 is occupying half the staff, I'm the only attending physician in the trauma bay. I have to float between these two patients.

I focus my attention on the woman and take a closer look at her leg while the techs cut the clothes off the older man in the bed next to us. The trauma residents begin their "primary survey" examination, and the emergency medicine resident stands at the head of the bed ready for any airway issues. Simultaneously, a nurse starts an IV, another takes the patient's blood pressure, and a third stands at a computer documenting what we're doing. The pharmacists prepare pain medications, drugs for resuscitation, sedatives, and paralytics from their red tackle box, which is equipped to address any emergency. Two techs are a blur of activity, cutting off clothes, covering the woman with a warm blanket, applying monitor leads, and finding gauze for the wound. All the while, I continue my examination. I discover that the woman has a single bullet wound that shattered her tibia—the large bone in her shin—and broke her fibula—the smaller bone. She'll need surgery to repair her fragmented leg sometime in the next twenty-four hours, but she has no other injuries.

I turn to the next bed and see that the older gentleman is in more trouble. Now that it's exposed, I can see that his right leg was previously amputated below the knee and that the left one is causing him pain near his hip. He's having trouble breathing and suffering with chest pain. After we measure his vital signs, get an IV started, and draw blood, we give him fentanyl for the pain and send him to the CT scanner to check for internal injuries. In the meantime, we move the younger woman out of the trauma bay to free up room in the ER.

When I engage the most intense situations and the sickest patients, I turn off my brain. Then experience, training, and time-tested algorithms transform complicated scenarios into simple steps. COVID forces me to rework my usual choreography for new music. I slow down to find my footing as I think through every situation. Keeping the team safe and PPE vigilance preoccupy thoughts that are usually free. Where usually there's no room for anxiety, now I'm nervous about making a mistake or taking too long with my new procedures.

We're still moving smoothly through the choreography of trauma, executing without thinking. But I can see that the new PPE and distance guidelines are causing little lapses in our execution. I find it as uncomfortable as brushing my teeth left-handed.

The changes are everywhere. We used to snack and sip throughout our shift to relieve stress and hydrate, but that's over. To eat or drink requires a sequence of unmasking, hand-washing, and finding a nonclinical area six feet away from anyone else. Once there, we've got to make sure that the food and beverages are safe and that we have PPE ready for when we're done. It's exhausting. But so is dehydration.

With the trauma bay settled I return to the COVID treatment area. I try to see my colleagues through my mask and through theirs, but even as I joke around with the nurses and techs as usual between patients, everything feels like it's happening across a murky fog of distance. A quiet feeling of alarm at this alien environment pulses through me. Once I take stock of who is here, I realize half of the usual staff is missing. There are fewer residents. The registration staff who usually greet me on the way in are gone. Respiratory therapists are not around, and neither are consultant physicians. The skeleton crew is the product of simple math: fewer opportunities to be infected should lead to fewer infected workers. I also learn that most of the doctors in the hospital are afraid to come down to the Emergency Department, the most infectious and uncontrolled area of the medical center. Their fear is also a rational calculation.

But for me, being in the ER feels better than being out in the city. Here there is a sense of control, but back in the real world things seem to be falling apart with every news update and email. Here our risk is in the patient room and with each adjustment of our PPE. In grocery stores nobody wears a mask, and every cough is like a bomb going off.

My next patient is an asthmatic who does not have a fever, runny nose, cough, or any other COVID symptoms. She's about twenty-eight and rail-thin, wearing a burgundy leather jacket. Her hair is dyed blond but seems like it hasn't been styled since she began having trouble breathing days ago. I stand close to the door fiddling with my empty hands that normally hold a stethoscope. I speak deliberately and loudly so that she can hear me through my mask.

"How do you feel, ma'am?"

Unable to speak, she just gives a thumbs-down. She holds her hands on her knees and her entire body tenses and releases with each breath in and out. In normal times I would give this young, otherwise healthy woman prednisone tablets and nebulized albuterol, and we'd watch her for a few hours until she felt well enough to go home. But now nebulized albuterol is off-limits; it aerosolizes coronavirus and puts everybody at risk. Instead, we offer albuterol inhalers, like the ones you can get at home, but—a week into the change—we are running out of the inhalers. To stretch the supply, we clean them after each use and use them with multiple patients. The washing cannot guarantee that they won't spread the virus to an uninfected patient, so we reserve inhalers for patients with COVID. Our treatment for asthmatics without COVID symptoms has regressed to treatments we used in 1970: terbutaline inhaler, theophylline pills, and epinephrine injections. These are messy drugs with tough side effects, and neither I nor my residents have any experience with them. But they work, and we catch on quickly. We prescribe this young woman an injection of epinephrine, prednisone, and theophylline tablets and move on.

A tall security guard with cornrows whom I can't recognize beneath his mask and goggles walks over to my work area, where I sit entering notes on the computer. He tells me that the woman who had been shot in her leg—her name is Janet, it turns out—has a family member in the waiting room. I adjust my eye protection and make sure my ID is visible before I go out to talk to her. She's a woman in her seventies wearing a procedure mask, a brown wig that is slightly askew, and a navy blue down coat. She's rummaging in an overflowing leather purse when I approach her.

"Hello, ma'am, are you with Janet?"

She stops fumbling and sits up.

"Yeah, I'm her mother." She speaks with a deep smoker's rasp.

"I'm Dr. Fisher, I've been taking care of her. She's doing fine."

Janet's mom nods and holds eye contact. I'm slightly unnerved by her gaze but continue.

"She has a wound to her leg that needs surgery tomorrow. But right now, she's comfortable."

"Thank God! Can I see her?"

"I'm sorry, we are not allowing any visitors back. It's a new rule, to protect visitors and patients."

This mom in particular cannot afford to be infected. Her apparent age puts her at high risk of death.

"Okay," she says, disappointment shading her voice. "Just tell her I love her."

I return to the ER and find Janet browsing through her phone on a gurney in Room 16 with her leg in a splint. When I relay her mother's message, she breaks down sobbing.

"I want to see my mommy."

Janet needs to be cared for, not just treated, and nobody cares better than her mother. Janet asks whether I can pass her mom a note, but her mother's already left, so I recommend Face-Timing her on her phone.

That is our new process. Janet slumps back on her gurney, her leg elevated on a folded blanket, fingers tapping out a message on her phone.

I walk to my next patient in Room 27, where the senior resident, Angelique, greets me at the door and in her presentation warns that the patient—in her forties and short of breath—has symptoms consistent with COVID. I find the patient fully dressed on the gurney in gray leggings and a striped brown sweater. She's wearing heavy eye makeup and a yellow mask that is covering her mouth but not her nose. Her eyes size me up under furrowed brows. When I ask what's going on, she begins her story over a year ago, when she began coughing and having trouble breathing.

"I was visiting family in Birmingham last Easter when I first started coughing."

While she rambles on, I stand close to the door and listen with my arms crossed over my yellow gown. Even covered in full protective equipment, I find myself creating as much distance as possible.

Her story, punctuated by coughs and throat-clearing, continues with expressive eye and arm movements. With every cough I can almost see the droplets spraying through the room— a mild panic starts to rise in me, and I want to let her finish her story, but the story keeps going. When she pauses, I try to focus her attention.

"If this started last year, what made today the day to come see about it?"

"I'm trying to tell you, just give me a second."

Another five minutes of coughing, throat-clearing, and rambling pass, and she has yet to get to the point of her current visit. When she pauses again, I jump in, trying to control my tone.

"I'm sorry that you've been ill so long, but did something change this week that made you come in?"

She restarts her story, this time beginning two years ago. "I'm trying to get to the past few days," she says. "Just let me talk." Now she lowers her mask so she can speak more clearly.

Without thinking I bark, "Mask on!" and she's jolted from her story. Rolling her eyes, she raises her mask and continues her digressive account. I interrupt again when she takes a pause and ask specific questions: "Were you feeling better at all in the last two weeks? When did this cough start? Do you have a fever? Who is sick at home?"

"I was feeling fine until a week ago when my family had a barbecue. My brother and son were coughing. Two days later I began coughing, and then two days after that I had a fever." She lets me know she's sure it's not coronavirus because, "as I've been trying to tell you, I've been sick for a very long time. Just on and off."

At that point she again lowers her mask, and I again direct her, "Mask up!" Denials aside, she has all of the hallmarks of "the Cove," as we call it now, and speaking for an extended period without her mask only spreads virus. I don't like to address patients so sharply, but her rambling story and sloppiness with her mask are creating a real risk for me and her nurse. Standing near unmasked COVID patients feels like being in the room with someone holding a gun.

She lifts her mask again and says defensively, "Well, I'm just trying to tell you." I soften my tone and try to reassure her, but there's really no middle ground here. She's got to keep her mask on. I tell her, "I'm sorry, I'm just trying to stay safe and keep you safe. You very likely have coronavirus, and if you don't, you might catch it here."

Her eyes look pained. I go on.

"You have classic symptoms. You're fortunate to be well enough to go home, but you have to tell people you probably have coronavirus, and you have to stay inside for two weeks."

Her eyes widen. "I'm not going to tell anybody! But I will stay home. I can't let anybody know that I have *it*." There is already such stigma associated with this plague. People know that if you are sick, you become a pariah—nobody will come near you for who knows how long. You will be alone. I don't know what to do about that. We don't have tests yet, so I can't even confirm that she's got COVID. I try to focus on the things she can control and reassure her that the huge majority of patients get better in a week or two.

"A lot of people here have coronavirus," I tell her as I'm being called out of the room. "You're not alone."

I'm now rushing to Room 41 with Roy, a second-year resident. Roy is a tall Kenyan with a dry sense of humor and a sharp mind, but for now we're both silent, moving quickly to get to a critical patient. The patient is a twenty-two-year-old woman who called 911 because of trouble breathing. She's plump with baby weight—she delivered just three days prior—and is sitting bolt upright, sweating profusely, and breathing so fast she can barely speak. Before we enter the room, we change out of regular masks into powered air-purifying respirators, cover our blue scrubs with a yellow gown, and put on blue gloves. The PAPR helmet filters the air of all particles and viruses, but the problem is once you have it on, it's very difficult to hear or be heard. It takes precious time to get on all our gear, so once we're in the room we need to move quickly—she can't last long breathing this hard. We prepare with such focus that I forget the dread that's been with me all shift.

In normal times this is a relatively straightforward case: we would support her breathing with mask ventilation and then test for common diagnoses like pulmonary embolism or post-partum cardiomyopathy. But the mask ventilator is off-limits because of COVID, so our choices are limited: we can either intubate her, which is a risky aerosolizing procedure and takes up a ventilator we might need for a COVID patient, or try to manage her with medication alone. Two nurses share the room with us, wearing N95 masks, goggles, and hair covers. Just outside the room, in the antechamber, there is another protected nurse on a walkie-talkie recording medications and communicating with us. She can relay our requests to the rest of the team standing just outside the antechamber. There wait a respiratory therapist, an X-ray technologist, an EKG tech, and a pharmacist ready to provide us what we need.

But what do we need?

The beauty of emergency medicine is the way an entire team can enter a flow state—perfect immersion and focus with no gap between thought and action. Rapidly evolving conditions synchronize my mind, words, and hands into fluid activity. But there's a dangerous flip side to the flow state: sometimes the patients flow, too—individuals turn into a blur of symptoms that need diagnosing, urgent problems that need fixing, impossible circumstances that need unraveling, and impediments to getting to the *next* patient. I see a patient and know that they are having a terrible day—I know that they are bewildered, often, or sometimes they are all too knowing. I see myself reflected in their eyes—when I allow it: I am flowing, but they want to be something more than a blur. They want me to pause for a moment. They need me to stop. This—as much as treatment—is what they've been waiting all these hours for. Patients with a doctor are said to be in the act of being *seen*. "She's being seen by a heart specialist." But do I "see" them? How can I make it clear, in the flow, in the constant movement, that they are real to me? That we are here together. They need to be seen, and I need to see them just as badly.

But time. Time doesn't allow it. They have so many questions, sometimes spoken, sometimes implicit: *How did this happen to me? Why am I suffering like this? How can I make it stop? And who, exactly, are* you, *this stranger standing so close, touching me,* seeing *me, this stranger I suddenly* need. I want to answer them. But there's no time.

Sometimes I imagine taking their names and addresses and writing them letters with all of the answers I didn't have time to give them in the rush of the emergency room. But for now, our time will be spent in a different way.

We direct the pharmacist to prepare intubation medications, and we set up the tubes, scopes, and bags that will be necessary to perform the procedure. But before we intubate, we try to help the young woman's breathing with medications: a large dose of a diuretic, Lasix, and another medication, nitroglycerin, that will reduce her blood pressure. Roy and I resolve to wait twenty minutes to see if it works before taking steps that are even more invasive.

Watching her labor to breathe is agonizing. She's panting with the intensity of someone who has sprinted, but without the promise of recovery with rest. With each cycle of inhale and exhale I search for the stare into infinity that leads out of consciousness and sometimes to death. We reassure her with calming words, dab her sweat, and find the best position to relieve her discomfort. The pharmacist, nurses, and techs can't stand the wait. They know that normally we would actively intervene to slow her huffing; for them, reassuring words while waiting on the medications to work are not enough for a life on the edge—we should *do something*. I can feel the team's impatience. At five and ten minutes they prompt us to just go ahead and put her on a ventilator. But we know one of the nearby hospitals is out of ventilators, and a second hospital has only three left. If we can save this woman without putting her on a ventilator it will be better for her, but it might also save another patient. On the other hand, if we wait too long and she dies from our delay, will we be able to keep the confidence of our team, who thought that we needed to intervene earlier? Hell, will we be able to forgive ourselves? While her diagnosis is unclear, her blood gas is reassuring, and she's young enough to withstand this strenuous period. It's my job to make the call, and my decision is to wait.

As we near the twenty-minute mark, she gasps that she needs to pee. Her sweat is drying, and her breathing has slowed. An X-ray of her chest shows fluid in her lungs. This could be coronavirus, but heart failure from postpartum cardiomyopathy looks similar. We press on with our course and give her magnesium and more Lasix and increase her dose of nitroglycerin. Another ten minutes pass, and she appears even more stable. Now she can talk again. The tension is broken, and with her improvement the nurses and techs calm. I let Roy know I'm stepping out. I move into the antechamber to break free from my PPE and wash before exiting into the hallway.

Thirty minutes later a fifty-nine-year-old man comes in breathing so hard you can hear him struggling from across the department. He has a left ventricular assist device implanted to support his failing heart. It is embedded in his abdomen and is hooked to his great vessels to circulate blood. He also has a permanent IV line that he'd been using for antibiotics at home. His sunken eyes are yellow, and his ribs are apparent under his skin. He wears a trucker hat and can barely catch his breath, sputtering one or two words at a time. Dan, his resident, and I enter the room in full protective gear. Dan's in his second year of training, but his prior life as a management consultant still influences his approach—a big-picture thinker who's adept with checklists. With hand motions and shrugs the patient lets us know that he's been breathing hard for two days and didn't notice that his eyes had yellowed—a sign commonly associated with liver damage. He's on the edge—he needs to be intubated and put on life support before we can establish what is causing his problem.

Unlike the recent mother I'd just seen, this man is not strong enough to fight for breath, and the low oxygen level in his blood gas test is ominous. So many things can go wrong with this ventricular assist device: Is it infected or clotted? Is it malfunctioning? Is this coronavirus? We can't know any of these answers soon enough, so we act. I instruct the pharmacist outside the room to prepare intubating drugs, and Dan assembles the tools to manage the man's airway. While setting up we share with the patient details of what is about to happen. He's so tired he stammers out, "Let's get . . . on . . . with it . . . hurry up. . . . Just give . . . me . . . the drugs."

We push medications through his IV that first sedate and then paralyze him. Dan uses a video laryngoscope to visualize his glottis and then passes a tube between his vocal cords and into his trachea. The intubation goes smoothly, but our sedatives are not effective in keeping him deeply sedated, and with closed eyes he fidgets on the gurney. He's critically ill and we still don't know if this is or isn't coronavirus. We increase his sedation with propofol, dose him with antibiotics, and prepare to admit him to the critical care unit.

It's been eight hours, and my shift is finally ending. I go to the locker room and sit down for a moment, contemplating my new routine. To start, I wash my hands with soap and water, then wipe my accessories and phone with a chlorhexidine swab. Then I wash my hands again, this time with alcohol-based gel, and remove my hospital scrubs. Wash again with alcohol, then put on my outside clothes and pack my bag. Eight hours of repeated handwashing has made my hands rough and itchy. When I finally take my mask off, my face is a wreck. My lips are chapped and swollen, and the mask and hair coverings have etched red furrows across my nose and forehead. My mouth is dry and my eyes sunken by dehydration. Taking care not to release any virus trapped in my clothes, I move slowly and deliberately. After returning the hospital scrubs to the scrub machine, I wash my hands a final time before exiting the ER through the waiting room into the night. I see that the temporary parking lot across the street is empty, and to my right the moon hovers over the main hospital building. A deep breath of cold air reassures me that I'm back on dry ground after a dive into the deep. I toss the mask in the overflowing garbage can outside the ED and then guzzle the bottle of water waiting for me in the car.

3

Dear Janet,

We met only briefly. I held your leg, ordered your pain medication, and stood between you and your mother. I was the strange man behind the mask and goggles who stood anonymously at your bedside on the day you were shot. I was your doctor, but only for a moment. It was probably not the first time we crossed paths, but you won't recognize me the next time we bump into each other on the Red Line or at Walgreens. I was wearing an official badge, which makes it hard to distinguish me from this institution. And the nature of our meeting means that I know more about you than you know about me. But we are from the same community and were joined in a pivotal moment in your life, and I want to introduce myself. You were brought into that room by the violence that rains on the city we share. I was, too.

I was nine years old when Ben Wilson was murdered. Do you remember that? Benji, as he was affectionately known, was the best high school basketball player in the country. He was tall, handsome, charismatic, and from the South Side of Chicago. It was 1984. Michael Jordan had been drafted by the Chicago Bulls a few months earlier and was dropping 28 a game. Jordan's exploits were filling the front page of the *Chicago Sun-Times*, and Benji's achievements blanketed the back. Jordan's number 23 was becoming iconic to kids on the playground. Benji's 25 a close second. Benji balled at Simeon High School, only a couple miles from where I lived with my family. He started as a sophomore and led his team to the state championship the next year. His play in the summer leagues led scouts to tout him as the best high school player in the country. In Benji, I envisioned my future. Maybe I could be first at something? It wasn't just me; Benji's rising star illuminated parts of our city that had long been shrouded in shadows.

In the fall of that year Benji walked out of Simeon with his girlfriend, accidentally bumped into a boy from a rival school, and was shot right there on the street. The shooting didn't just kill Benji; it also changed me. Now the idea of murder transformed from theoretical and distant—something that happened on the evening news—to something that could happen to me, to anyone. Benji was being groomed to excel, as was I—but for me it wasn't in basketball, it was in academics. His parents were professionals, like mine. He had been sheltered from the streets, just as I was being protected. I was taught that the world was wide, and I could be anything, being prepared for departure in the same way that Benji was. But before Benji was able to leap from the community into the world, it all ended.

Benji was taken to St. Bernard Hospital, not far from here, in the Englewood neighborhood. According to the news there he lay on a gurney in shock for hours before he was taken to surgery. Reportedly his life slipped away as his care team dithered. Benji's injury—a .22 gunshot to the abdomen—did not need to kill him. We are only a few blocks away from where he was shot, and even then the University of Chicago Medical Center had more modern facilities, better trained surgeons, and more of them. Perhaps they would have taken a different course, and he could have lived. Life and death for Benji were determined by a hot-headed teenager, the paramedics' selection of the closest hospital, and the decisions of unprepared surgeons. Different choices by any of those people could have delivered Benji from danger and made the confrontation a violent footnote to his life's trajectory. It was decades before I understood each of these what-ifs in their appropriate context.

I remember the grief that befell Chicago. Both strangers and loved ones wept at his funeral, which was televised. Tears streamed down the twisted faces of grieving teens who hugged in groups of three or four. Benji's mother never cracked. Her stoic speech was interrupted by the wails of youths who'd lost not only their friend but a source of great pride as well. Their prince was gone. His mother's resolve in those moments reminded me of my own mother when she commanded resources for neglected children in the school she worked at as a social worker. Her style was not that different from what I observed in your mom when I met her in the waiting room. In a televised interview, flanked by Jesse Jackson, Benji's mom said she hoped that his death meant something, that his life would lead to safer streets, that no other children would be killed. While that was my first brush with murder, violence would be nearby for the rest of my life.

Janet, there are probably many similarities in our lives, if we are both the children of this neighborhood. But I'm sure there are differences, too—so many of us are descendants of the Great Migration, of poor Black folks looking for something better, looking to escape Southern poverty and terrorism. But even then, there are so many paths into and out of and through this neighborhood.

I grew up in a red brick townhouse complex on a tree-lined street in Hyde Park, a couple miles from the hospital where Benji succumbed. It is one of Chicago's few racially integrated enclaves on the densely segregated and mostly Black South Side. There was a Mexican-Lebanese family on one side of us and a white Jewish family on the other. Our household of five lived in a ground floor unit of a sixty-four-unit residential complex. Summer thunderstorms sometimes flooded the bottom floor, and the Number 6 bus rumbling past rattled glasses on the kitchen table. Our living room had ficus plants and African masks my uncle brought from Senegal. Every Sunday I had to Windex the glass coffee tables, clean the bathrooms, and take out the garbage. Dutch elm disease destroyed the shade trees on my block. Now, thirty-five years later, the frail honey locust trees of my childhood are tall enough to cool the sidewalks.

Two blocks down, a pandemonium of green parakeets lived in the park. Their nests were a nimbus of twigs that dominated two trees. The green birds screeched in competition with pigeons for crumbs. Rumor was they had escaped from an experiment at the University of Chicago and feasted on garbage to survive the winter. These birds flew with me as I walked to Pat the butcher on the corner. He knew my order of three whole chickens, cut up, as soon as I walked in. I'd watch his cleaver's speed and precision and then lug them home. Oprah had just come to a local affiliate, and Jesse Jackson was preparing a run for the White House when Chicago elected our first Black mayor. Harold Washington's apartment surveyed the park, right across the street from those parakeet nests. His security detail watched as I learned how to ride a bike. We had great pride that the mayor lived right down the street. We also welcomed the new streetlights and the prompt snowplowing.

My parents are first-generation Chicagoans. Their meeting was engineered by a nurse at Henry Ford Hospital in Detroit, where my father interned. That nurse was my mom's aunt, and a blind date led to a relationship. When his internship ended and he moved to Chicago for residency, they faced a crossroads. According to the story, she would not move without a ring. When that ring materialized, they raised a family on the South Side of Chicago. He drew on his Kansas roots and transformed the corner of an empty lot into a small garden plot for watermelon, greens, and onions. His orientation was toward hard work, solutions to problems, and facts. That made him seem naive in a city full of hustlers, but he was always productive. Mom landed a role as a Chicago Public Schools social worker. She joined a produce co-op and exposed us to new fruit each summer. Her identity is tied to justice, protecting the least among us, and finding joy in any situation. She seems like a dreamer in a city full of suffering, but she was the light in all of our lives. Photos from that time show a loving couple, Mom with reddish curls, Dad in his Army Reserve jacket, the two of them hugging on the Midway.

My father was the fourth of five children raised by Beulah and Charles in Kansas. His brother, Charles Jr., the eldest of the Fisher children, spent most of his life in a sanatorium after being diagnosed with tuberculosis during his childhood. Charles would come home on occasion, but my grandparents kept him away from the younger children to avoid "the consumption." Then, when he turned eighteen, Charles was taken to the University of Kansas Medical Center to have a lung, or part of a lung, removed. No one in the family is sure how it happened, but Charles died either in surgery or during recovery. It's a mystery how Junior died or whether he even needed the procedure. For all their resourcefulness and knowledge of the land, my grandparents had little education, and in Jim Crow Kansas, Black families didn't enjoy a participatory health-care experience. My father remembers my grandmother weeping at the funeral. And he recalls her tears when, years later, he earned his medical degree from the same University of Kansas.

His parents lived lean and rarely saw vacation. My grandmother was a robust, stout woman who kept the home. It's hard to recognize her in photos, as she always seemed to be shrouded in a large dress and wearing a scowl, but the grandma I knew shared a ready laugh and plenty of lessons. My grandfather operated an elevator at a meat-packing company and died when I was two. In photos, he wears denim overalls and a part in his hair, and he never smiled. During the summer my parents and siblings would drive through a network of Midwestern highways and off-ramps until we reached a long gravel road. Then we'd motor past plots of trees and over a creek until we reached my grandparents' single-story home with a large back porch overlooking their acre plowed for peas, okra, tomatoes, and potatoes. During the day my older sister and I would play tag, pull weeds, and turn over stones to see what was crawling under them. At night we'd listen to cicadas and scratch mosquito bites. The blackberry bushes and grapevines were closest to the house and the chicken coop nearest the road. One summer when I was about eight, while I was playing in the garden near the potatoes, my grandma came out of the house with a 20-gauge shotgun. When she blasted into her lettuce patch, a rabbit leapt into the air, landed twitching. An hour later it was in her iron skillet smothered with gravy.

Like many raised in Jim Crow, my father's earliest memories are of learning rules. While my grandparents' formal education ended before the eighth grade and resources were scarce, they were curious, engaged, and ingenious. They raised five kids with an understanding of farming, animal husbandry, and crafts. Children were not to speak until spoken to, there were daily chores in the home, and cutting corners meant a whipping. When he started at the integrated high school, my dad recalls being told by his father to "leave the white girls alone." Those rules, authoritarian and unforgiving, saved him. His faithful adherence to spoken and unspoken directions guided his path from rural, segregated Kansas to a life in Chicago.

Jim Crow marked my mother's life as much as my father's. Her greatest lesson was through stories of my Grand-Uncle Ivory. He was described as a charming young man with wavy hair, a casual swagger, and green eyes, and girls in his hometown of Valdosta, Georgia, loved him—perhaps the wrong kind of girls. I've heard the day of his disappearance was the same day my grandmother left for Detroit. That's probably an exaggeration, but it is clear his lynching over the attention of a white woman set the stage for their migration north. From what my mother passed to me, Georgia meant living by white people's demands to step aside, to pay more, and to live less energetically. When Grand-Uncle Ivory disappeared, they set their sights on Detroit and migrated to where my mother was raised. In the summer of 2018, my mother and I searched for Uncle Ivory's name on a plaque at the National Memorial for Peace and Justice in Alabama. As for so many people memorialized there for simply living, terrorism shaped the life course of Black folks in my family.

The oldest of four, my mother was reared in segregation on the northwest side of Detroit, in a vast Black middle class born of union work on automobile assembly lines. Like my father, she was raised in a world of rules: be on time and well groomed, use frequent *pleases* and *thank-you*s. Instructions to keep the nuns at her Catholic elementary school from whacking her thighs, policies to make sure shopkeepers dealt with her fairly, and guides to keep the police billy clubs off her brothers' backs.

In photos, my grandmother on my mother's side was tall and

brown with a cheerful smile while my grandfather was thin, light-skinned with wavy hair. He appeared white. Granddad fought in the Battle of the Bulge and brought back both Nazi paraphernalia and nightmares from combat. Returning to an America no better than the one he left, he was able to attend law school on the GI Bill because he could pass for white. After graduating from the University of Detroit law school, he married my grandmother, a schoolteacher and later a principal. When my grandfather died prematurely, my mother, only fifteen, stepped in to help my grandmother lead the household. Mom and her three brothers all earned college degrees. Becoming a masters-prepared social worker, she devoted her life to the social and emotional development of children in the direst situations.

Working with children trapped by circumstances, my mother saw clearly how society kills, rapes, and imprisons its most vulnerable. That for some people struggle is unrelenting, and if there is any safety, it comes from their community. Although she was an atheist, she brought us to church—not for religion but to learn our traditions, language, and styles. She made certain that we knew all the "Black Leaders" made famous by Black History Month quizzes, but beyond that she also elevated the Black people all around us, people we could see and touch, who were leading every day. When we'd walk by the pier, she'd point out the *African Queen,* a yacht reportedly owned by the *Ebony/Jet* family. We'd buy only Baldwin ice cream out of respect for its Black founders, who lived on the South Side. Soft Sheen was led by a family my parents knew, and its blue grease went in our hair. Ribs N' Bibs was not only on our table, but it sponsored the local Little League, and one of the proprietors' kids was on my team. We had a Black dentist, a Black orthodontist, a Black pediatrician, a Black pharmacist; our postman was Black, our fishmonger was Black, and so was the man at the shoe repair shop. None of this was accidental.

My parents' move to Chicago followed a well-trodden path for Black folks. Chicago was founded by a Black Haitian fur trader in about 1780. The Underground Railroad had routes right through the city. Still-standing institutions, like Olivet Baptist Church, fed and housed Black people fleeing bondage. Ida B. Wells found refuge in Chicago from the white mobs incensed by her exposé of lynchings in the South. Provident Hospital, founded by Daniel Hale Williams to train doctors and nurses, had anchored health care for Black folks on the South Side since 1891. Dr. Williams also founded the National Medical Association in response to the American Medical Association's systematic exclusion of Black doctors. On South 51st and East Forrestville Avenue, Provident was renowned for its care and stands a half mile from the University of Chicago Medical Center. My father retired from Provident Hospital in the late '00s, and I've been an attending at the University of Chicago since 2006.

The city's early Black population was dwarfed by the waves of Black folks who arrived during the Great Migration. Between 1916 and 1970 Chicago netted five hundred thousand Black people seeking jobs and fleeing white terrorism in the South. Coming north on trains and by foot, Black migrants settled in between 31st and 55th. That enclave along State Street and South Parkway sizzled with culture and commerce and anchored the South Side that later beckoned my parents. Jobs were in meatpacking houses, on trains as porters, and in the homes of white people, but Black people were excluded from living in white communities by restrictive covenants and redlines. Bricks, bottles, and bombs made sure no one tried to find loopholes in that strict segregation. After a while white people fled north and west within the city or followed the newly built highways, into the suburbs, ossifying segregation.

In 1969 *Dorothy Gautreaux et al. v. Chicago Housing Authority* forced the Chicago Housing Authority to abandon its discriminatory tenant assignment plan. No longer could the CHA assign all Black public housing residents to buildings in Black neighborhoods and white residents to buildings in white neighborhoods. But it was too late: high-rise housing projects were built almost exclusively in the city's Black communities. By the '70s more than a million Black people lived in dense segregation, where they and their neighbors were uniformly poor and separated from public services. Our community's segregation was built by decisions made just a couple generations ago.

Around here, Black people who were upper-middle-class had more poor neighbors, worse schools, and fewer health-care options than poor white people. By the time my parents arrived in 1970, the War on Drugs had been launched and was shackling men in Black Chicago with criminal records, pushing them out of the workforce. Predatory lending robbed families of wealth and ultimately their homes, leaving neighborhoods cluttered with abandoned buildings. Public and private disinvestment emptied communities of jobs—and the safety net. The solutions proposed by philanthropy emphasized "community development"—programs aimed at making ghettos more habitable rather than destroying segregation itself and freeing Black people once and for all. White conservatives favored these plans that kept Black folks where they were, white liberals liked the money that flowed in, and Black politicians prized the stable electoral base.

Today there simply aren't very many jobs available on the South Side, and the ones that do exist pay less money. Seven hundred thousand jobs are located within a thirty-minute train or bus ride from the largely white Loop and North Side, while only fifty thousand jobs are located within a thirty-minute commute from the heavily Black South Side. About 34 percent of Black people in Chicago earn less than half of the local minimum wage, cobbling together a living through the gig economy and part-time jobs. Black folks make up approximately one third of Chicago's population but almost 80 percent of the population of persistently low or volatile food-access areas.

In this desert we found oases. While guns were common, old housing was full of lead paint, and police executed Black men, the community still launched Katherine Dunham, Richard Wright, and Gwendolyn Brooks. Whether suited or in African garb, hair permed or locked, starter jacket or dinner jacket, all kinds of Black folks strutted on the South Side. My siblings and I were taught the rules to stay safe in an oppressive society, just as my mother and my father had been trained. In the short term that meant summers with grandparents and warnings about the way we conducted ourselves in public. Over the long term, we were admonished to build a safety net in preparation for the inevitable bad turns. A side hustle, something practical and portable to fall back on, was necessary if a precipitous migration became necessary. An uncle's conspiracy theory taught us to avoid settings that white institutions set aside for Black folks for fear of "secret societies" plotting against us. The importance of being twice as good as our white peers came from my grandmother. She drummed into us that we did not have the luxury of mediocrity like our white peers. Every Black friend I have received similar lessons, and all of us rolled our eyes as these lessons were repeated over our childhoods.

Integrated private elementary school taught me to think like white kids—to approach the world as though there were no boundaries and there was nothing to fear. We learned language through poetry, chemistry with bench experiments, and history from its authors. Music, art, and athletics were not sidelined, and humanities mattered as much as science. School came easily to me. I picked up reading quickly, was a good test taker and a versatile athlete, and felt confident in the classroom. My peers saw me as a leader even if I was unnecessarily competitive. Private education was a financial burden, as a result of which we never had new cars or trendy clothes; those were deemed unnecessary luxuries. Mom required that the subject of every assigned book report would be a Black person—exclusive of athletes. "Why do I have to do a report on Ralph Bunche when my friend gets to do Walter Payton?" I remember complaining. Those times were safe and simple but not separate from societal ordering. Those rules penetrated all aspects of my life.

In fifth grade, stratification began. Our love of Dungeons & Dragons led a substitute teacher to instruct on medieval times in order to maintain our attention. She asked the class, "Why is purple the royal color?" My Uncle Robert, the conspiracy theorist, schoolteacher, and later COVID victim, had taught me the answer while at a Detroit Tigers game the summer before. This sub ignored my raised hand until she'd called on every white child in the class, even those who were trying to avoid being picked out. We were left so stunned that the next day my classmate Susanna told our teacher about the incident and asked to keep that sub from returning. By sixth grade the Black table emerged in the lunchroom, racially configuring our previously tight group for good.

That summer between sixth and seventh grade, I showed up at a church in Park Manor with hundreds of other Black kids for summer camp. Boom boxes filled the streets with UTFO and Newcleus. Air Jordans were on every foot, and the jolt of Benji's death was starting to fade. One day we took a field trip to the Field Museum of Natural History. This place had a preserved five-foot-long coelacanth—still does—which made it my favorite museum in the city. Trips with my private school were led by docents who described how coelacanths linked marine and terrestrial evolution. That summer we never saw the coelacanth, and rather than encourage our curiosity, the docent made sure we didn't touch anything and stayed together. Our questions went unanswered, and her look of suspicion was new to me. Rather than the usual Field Museum experience of wolf hunt dioramas and whales breaching, it was my first experience of being policed.

Policing intensified in high school. I attended my neighborhood public high school; with two thousand kids, Kenwood Academy took up an entire city block. The high school reflected the neighborhood: bougie kids and dope boys, students headed to Harvard, and others just trying to get through the day. We had a state championship academic decathlon team, and we were barred from playing football against our rival, Whitney Young, after the shooting that followed the last game. At the start and end of every school day, Blackstone Avenue, the street that ran in front of the school, thumped with bass from cars and the shouts of kids greeting or leaving each other. Our hallways were rife with budding entrepreneurs selling candy, T-shirts, spare Coach tags, and answers for the test. Within a week of starting, I was introduced to the challenge of calculating integers and computing the safest way home.

Sorry for the long digression, Janet, but to the point: violence always returns. It is always with us. In the spring of my sophomore year, my good friend Larry was killed. We ran track together, and he was the fastest dude I ever met. As his senior year wound down, he lolled away his days entertaining various scholarship offers. I had just

worked my way onto the varsity 4x100 relay team after a strong in-
door season. My job was not to lose our position in the third leg, hand
Larry the baton, and watch him eat up the competition. "Go!" sig-
naled when to start sprinting and "Swat!" meant it was time to reach
back for the baton. I was anxious to get to practice. We had no track,
so when the weather was below 50 degrees we practiced in the hallways. Running inside was complicated by the fumes of cleaning solutions and floors so slick we had to slow down to take a corner. To
whip those suburban kids who competed in new running spikes, we
had to practice our baton handoff. That spring day we had a suburban track meet coming, and we carried our relay batons with us in the
hallway between classes and yelled "Swat!" if we saw one another.
That day Larry was nowhere to be found. We went through our paces
without him, muttering about our missing anchor. This wasn't the first
time he had skipped practice—senioritis had a hold of him. The track
coach threatened to suspend him.

It was the next day that we learned Larry was dead. He had been
chilling outside school on 51st and got into an altercation over shoes—
or was it a girl? While we were in the locker room getting changed for
practice, he was shot. He died a few hours later. I was dazed. I had
just seen him, and we had plans. We were going to win the relay
downstate. I was going to ask him how to get out of the blocks faster.
He was real one day but just stories and memories the next. The
school shrugged. We were told, he's an example of why we shouldn't
hang out after school, and that was it. No counseling, no therapy, and
no one asked whether we were okay. I didn't stick with track that year
but returned for junior and senior years. It was a while before I told my
parents—they were worried enough, and no mother can protect a
fifteen-year-old in the Chicago Public Schools. Neither parent was

able to advise or shelter me at a time when the city's streets were slick with blood.

I struggled to reconcile this world of murdered classmates. The Nation of Islam's self-sufficiency (and antisemitism) saw self-segregation as a way to keep our community together and safe from phantom white devils. Black strivers proclaimed that working hard, following rules, and being better than white people was the way to safety and prosperity. Black nationalists taught me that we came from kings and queens and that I had to rely on myself, know our culture, and live alongside this culture of oppression without being shackled by it. The church community taught me to surrender, give it to God, and know there's always a plan. Hustlers said to hell with all that, getting over is the American way, go and make it happen. Rise and grind. I tried on all these ideas.

In private school, I'd been in a place where resources were abundant, words were kind, bad manners were reinforced, and policing was absent. At Kenwood, mere blocks away, that setting seemed like a foreign country. There, police colors struck fear, and violence occupied half my brain space—by this time I knew too well that minor mistakes could lead to disqualification, incarceration, maybe even death. I gathered that safety was not contingent on the way I behaved. No matter whether my pants were pulled up or if I made "good" decisions, at all times I was subject to the whims of power and the blade of violence. There was no easy way to protect myself or my friends. To stay safe and move forward, I was required to calculate solutions to equations with inputs that were out of my control.

I cried when I graduated. In 1992 there were 942 people murdered in Chicago, 201 more than the year Benji was killed, and the all-time high. I was ready to leave for college. The South Side taught me values of service, responsibility, and compassion. I side-hustled my way to reasonable skills cutting hair, which provided an extra buck in college and now keeps my line tight even as we practice social distancing. My uncle's conspiracy theories made me suspicious of conspiracies in general. I demanded facts rather than accept an unseen illuminatus, but in a country where the government could poison the water in Flint, Michigan, I also understood why people think HIV is manmade. My grandmother's lessons on being twice as good pushed me to have strong grades balanced with athletics. Now that lesson is a reminder of a basic injustice: Black folks aren't allowed human foibles and flaws, triumphs and humiliations. The lessons from my Grammy, a Black woman born in 1916, helped me see how Donald Trump could become president of the United States.

I did not look back when I stepped out of my parents' minivan at college. Hanover, New Hampshire, was a three-stoplight town in Norman Rockwell's New England, but even here I was anxious to explore adulthood. Home to wealthy prep school kids, with breezes scented by pine, Hanover had no sirens and no worry about weapons. I found community with dudes from the Bronx whose Fresh Air Fund experiences shaped their childhood, Canadian West Indians who introduced me to mauby, and brothers from the South who had never seen snow. I had the confidence of youth and enough preparation to back it up. I jumped into class work anxious to test myself.

Claustrophobia descended quickly. Our community of Black and brown people was so small that I'd met everyone within eight weeks. The dominant language and customs on campus left few ways for Black men to be themselves. Invited speakers and concerts rarely held relevance to our cultural lives. Few mentors related to our trajectories out of cities into the woods. Any small stumble sent folks home. Black men were kicked out for low grades, public intoxication, or dorm fights, and many never returned, but somehow drunk and rapey frat boys floated along untouched. Numbing our bewilderment with alcohol, marijuana, or harder things put us at even higher risk of a precipitous exit. These experiences prepared me for a professional life in the halls of traditional power where Black men have a separate set of rules and pressures.

I put myself and my parents in debt for this experience. Living a world away, in a place where anything seemed possible, I was going to make the most of it, one way or another. I lived with a French family in Lyon for language study abroad, cleaned my Air Force 1s for Fashion Friday while on exchange at Morehouse, and gawked at Biggie on the DC Armory stage for Howard's homecoming weekend. My grades went up and down with my moods and whether my friends were present or absent from campus. I struggled and soared over those four years, in the process building a record sufficient to earn admission to medical school.

Four years flashed by. Our commencement speaker emphasized how very easy it is to be a critic and how difficult to build something. Despite a growing track record of success, I regularly doubted my ability. Sometimes I quit trying in the middle of things, preferring a mediocre outcome rather than face failure without a ready-made excuse. Improving skills, clarifying motivation, and releasing fear: I wasn't yet ready for that kind of work—I still preferred the comfort of the sidelines over sweating in the arena. This inclination led me to drop a class midway through senior spring that I thought was superfluous. An email two weeks before graduation notified me that the class was needed to graduate. After heated phone calls and dean's office meetings, they let me walk anyway, but I received no degree on graduation day. The leafy campus decked out for commencement and a medical school slot ahead should have made graduation a festival, but I was in no mood to celebrate. At graduation dinner with uncles, aunts, and both grandmothers who had come to celebrate, I went through the motions. My father was proud nonetheless and reminded me of the importance of building over criticizing. The sting of that unforced error pushed me to confront my approach, and his support and words focused me. I vowed to pursue goals doggedly. In medical school I would not stand in my own way.

I returned to the South Side for medical school at the University of Chicago. In Hanover if I walked ten minutes in any direction I'd end up in a forest. I had grown accustomed to living without looking over my shoulder, lost in whatever thoughts filled my head. I had to readjust to boundaries defined by struggle and violence. My default scowl returned, as did the daily deviations for the safest paths. One day while I was walking east down 56th Street a med school classmate's cheery "Hi Tom!" jolted me from my street attitude to the practiced pose that comforts white folks. She gave me a big hug and mentioned how she wasn't sure it was me until I had gotten closer. While my world was ordered by segregation and navigating white spaces, my classmates didn't see these same barriers. My Chicago was bounded by Roosevelt on the north to 95th on the south, while my classmates went from Hyde Park to the city's museums and bars far north. I was invited to the steakhouses of River North and the music venues of Lakeview, places I previously considered out of bounds. I was an Ivy League graduate and in medical school; could I dare consume the city in the same way as other Ivy League graduates? Was North Michigan Avenue mine? Could I pop in and out of the shops of Lincoln Park?

My questions were answered in the summer of 1999. Twenty-two-year-old Robert Russ was killed weeks before his Northwestern University graduation when a Chicago police officer shot him dead in a traffic stop. Russ and I were both Black men, middle-class, and in school. At the time of his execution, Russ was a few years younger than me. We had never met, but his parents' news conference let me know that he had been twice as good, embraced his education, and followed the rules just as I had. He had been being prepared to succeed anywhere in the world, as had I. Yet he was not protected by his education or status, and so neither was I. Russ's parents cried over his casket rather than toasting his graduation. Chicago could never be fully mine. For old and entrenched reasons, we all had our places.

Janet, I'm so sorry about your leg. We both know what happened to you is not right and this is not the first brush with guns for either of us. Neither of us can bring back Larry, Robert, or Benji, nor can we undo your injury, but I'm doing my best to stop the bleeding and relieve your pain. I am here because I am directed by a family and a community that taught me I'm linked to something bigger, to a people that has been here on the South Side for more than a hundred years. My calling is to take care of people like Benji, people like Larry, people like Robert, people like you, folks struck by health-care emergencies in the same community that pushed and shaped me. By working right here, I can give oxygen to my sixth-grade gym teacher who is sick with cancer and help my friend navigate the convoluted system for his mom who has early dementia. You need to know this community, and you by extension, mean the world to me. Even when I'm frustrated and tired, even when you're mad at my hospital and me as its surrogate, we're still family.

Now that I've told you part of my story, maybe you recognize me and maybe my story is familiar to you. I bet I remind you of people in your family, or maybe you went to high school with people like me. I'm sure you know other folks who are committed to the South Side, who

take care of sick people and who see themselves as part of something bigger. Taking care of folks right here is my life's work. I share all
this because I want you to see me, just as I want to see you. We're
here together.

Onward,

tlf

4

NOVEMBER 2019
(Before COVID)

LEFTOVER ROAST CHICKEN IS warming in the oven, and I've got
kale braising on the stove. Today is a 6 P.M. to 2 A.M. shift. When
I work late, I carefully regiment the preceding day to steady the
fatigue and hunger that come with unusual hours. I learned
long ago that as my grind extends into the wee hours, cravings
fan frustration into anger and uncertainty into panic. So I go to
the grocery, take meetings, and work out, then at 2 P.M. I nap for
a couple of hours. I'm now up and prepping a large meal before
I head in. While not always successful, this routine gives me the
best shot at being the patient, curious, and loving doctor of my
aspirations. Protein and greens for now, carbs and caffeine to
settle hankerings later. Today I'm in gray scrubs with my name
embroidered in maroon across the right chest, a disposable pen
in my breast pocket, phone in my back pocket, and ID on my
collar. I hail a ride share early, expecting to be held up by rush
hour traffic.

I arrive as I always do, through the waiting room. To the left, in the area for parking wheelchaired patients, there are three rows of six people. Men and women, old and young, obese and thin, all bound tightly in puffy winter coats and knit hats. Some are slumped, with mouth agape; others are erect and staring at me intently as I walk past. All wear a weary mask. The rest of the waiting room is taken up by rows of maroon plastic and wire stackable chairs like you'd find in a church basement. Each one holds a bundled person. Some murmur to the individuals next to them, some drum their fingers, some have twisted faces, and a couple are speaking to the unseen. In the aisles between chairs folks pace around talking on their cell phones. A tense din floats over the room, but there are no shouts or confrontations right now. The Bulls game plays silently on two wall-hung TVs. We're losing.

I'm tasked to the rapid assessment unit (RAU) of the department. It is a frenzy of activity. The objective is to meet patients right after they're triaged by the nurse, start their care by ordering tests, and then direct them to the place in the ED where they'll have their problem treated. I cover six assessment bays with a team of nurses and techs and the help of a scribe, Evan, who documents my interactions with patients. My area is laid out with three bays on either side of a hallway, each with a recliner chair and closed by a curtain. I see patients in groups of three, then write orders, edit Evan's note, and decide where to guide them for their next steps. In a busy shift I'll see ten patients in an hour. While the math suggests each patient gets six minutes, each patient receives only a fraction of that time— I talk with them for three of those six minutes and then sit in front of a computer for the other three to order treatments and diagnostics and document the interaction. Three minutes is all I have to see the person in front of me.

Along the way the electronic medical record tracks the time it takes for a person to be seen by a doctor. Known as the "door-to-doctor" time, this quality metric elevates hospitals that see patients soon after they arrive. Hospitals that have a long "door-to-doctor" time are deemed to be of lower quality. By initiating testing and treatment in the rapid assessment unit, my interaction satisfies the "door-to-doctor" stopwatch. While I am the "doctor" captured in the report, the few minutes I give each patient barely qualifies as doctoring. I can't effectively examine patients when they're fully clothed in a chair. I don't have time to listen to their stories, and I rarely have the chance to relieve their pain. In this setting I can deliver only a fraction of the skills and insights that I have accrued in my decades of experience. Still, sometimes, even in that small window, I can find a threatening disorder and influence its outcome. For those with straight-forward complaints like a cold, rash, or sprain, I know with a little more time and a couple of extra resources I could solve their problem and send them on their way. When I can't or don't, it leaves us both frustrated.

Once past the waiting room, I land at my computer in the RAU and perform my ritual keyboard cleaning. After a few swipes with a disinfecting wipe, it's fresh, or at least fresh enough, and I begin the extended log-on sequence with one password after the next. Finally, I survey the landing screen of the electronic medical record, which is a track board of every registered patient in the entire ER. There are thirty-eight people waiting to be seen. A couple of them have been waiting six and a half hours.

Through the locked doors between the RAU and the waiting
room strides Craig the tech. He's in blue scrubs and has the bari-
tone and cadence of a preacher, and photos of his children are
tucked in front of the hospital ID that hangs around his neck.
We dap like the longtime colleagues that we are, and he asks me
how I am.

"I'm all good, my brother. You straight?"

"Proper like a whopper," he says, and then tells me about a
sixty-eight-year-old woman in the waiting room who has been
waiting five hours and whose son wants to take her home. I say,
"Let's go!" and trail Craig back through the locked doors to the
waiting area.

The triage nurse owns a semi-private cove in the waiting
room where they check in patients and assess their vital signs.
Before I meet the family, I nestle in behind the nurse and quickly
review the woman's labs ordered by the prior rapid assessment
doctor. It turns out she has kidney failure. Craig brings over the
older woman's son. His black beret leans to the side, and his
long black leather trench coat brushes the floor. "An old-school
pimp," by Craig's description.

"Aye, Doc, nice to meet you, nice to meet you."

"Good to meet you too, fam." With that we bump fists. "I
understand you want to take your mom home."

"Yeah, Doc. We been here five hours, we're tired. Why don't
we just come back tomorrow?"

I look over his shoulder but can't identify his mom among
the many people hunched in the rows of wheelchairs, but I
advise him not to go. "I just took a look at her labs, and she's
got some kidney trouble. It looks new. I know you've been
here a long time, and it's not right, but can you stay just a little

longer? It's important. We should really find out why her kidneys are damaged and try to reverse it. I can't promise how
much longer she'll wait, but I'll make her a priority." With his
hands on his hips, he sighs deeply, looks to the ceiling, and
nods okay.

I feel like I am abandoning him to a purgatory of more waiting. Five hours is too long. Heading back to the RAU, I pass my
desk, walk down the hall, and go directly to the charge nurse to
let her know about this patient and her kidney failure. Charge
pledges to elevate her status, but I know it may not make any
difference. All our beds are full, and after reviewing the other
patients who are waiting, even her life-threatening condition
might not make her the sickest person waiting for a room. That
gap between what we *need* to do for truly sick people and what
we *can* do because of resource constraints is one of the deepest
frustrations I face. My neck grows warm with the spark of irri-
tation, the exact emotion that I struggle to manage when I'm
hungry or tired. It's too early for this—I just got here. I take a
deep breath and try to quench that flicker of exasperation by
reminding myself that suffering is part of the human condition,
we're here doing our best. We pay attention to the "door-to-
doctor" time but what does that matter if we "see" patients
quickly and then fail to provide folks the care they require? Is
there a way to give people what they need, when they need it?
Every day I push the boulder; every day it rolls back.

"Today matters!" I repeat to myself every so often to ground
myself. Listening to nurses discuss how night shift is better than
day shift anchors me to something current, something tangible.
I'm back to my chair, my computer, and back to the grind. Evan
and I dive into the first three bays to meet patients waiting for

care. The first is a thirty-three-year-old woman in a pink and black hijab who says she's two months pregnant and has been bleeding for two days. This is her second pregnancy after an uneventful first one. Now her left side hurts, and she's concerned. I am too: this could be an ectopic, a life-threatening pregnancy where the embryo implants in the fallopian tubes instead of the uterus. When I press her stomach through her black shirt, she has no pain. I let her know we'll get a urine sample, blood tests, and an ultrasound as soon as we find her a room with a door. Three minutes.

Next is a forty-year-old healthy-looking man in a gray sweater, jeans, and polished brown boots. He says calmly that he's been bleeding when he has stools, four times already today. Out of his pocket he produces an iPhone photo of what looks like Thanksgiving cranberry sauce in a toilet. His vitals are normal, his countenance is calm, and he appears younger than his age. I let him know we'll draw blood and set him up in the specialty area of the department for a full exam. Three minutes.

The third is a twenty-seven-year-old man, dressed in Timberland boots and a puffy black winter coat, complaining of back pain. This is one of our ER's most common complaints. While nagging back pain is usually benign, I still have to sort through the garden-variety aches to find the ones that signal a kidney stone, spine infection, or aortic aneurysm. It hurts him when he moves, and he has no concerning signs. I order a pain-numbing patch and let him know we'll continue treating him in the low-acuity area, where we sew lacerations and wrap ankle sprains. Three minutes.

Each of these three interactions started the same way. "Hi, I'm Dr. Fisher, this is Evan, our scribe. We work as a team. He writes notes while we talk. So, tell me, what's going on? What brought you in?" Evan is a white dude in his twenties. He wears beige scrubs to distinguish him from the caregivers; we wear blue. Evan is always relaxed and ready, but we're not exactly friends—no banter, no chatter, just business. This combination makes us very productive together. After I see three patients, I spend the next nine minutes at the desk writing orders, editing and accepting his notes. It's efficient and sometimes mind-numbing. We get through patients quickly, but I rarely have time to probe patients with the more detailed questions that might unlock why now, why today, why they are *really* here. I almost always learn the obvious portions: where it hurts, what they've tried for it, what makes it worse. But I want to know the twists in the path that led them here, sitting in front of me in an ER bay for three minutes. Without these details, by the end of a four-hour block, patients start to blend together in my mind, and it becomes difficult to pick out a specific memory of more than a few of the thirty or forty people I've seen.

After that first group of three, I dash through my desk work, then I'm off to the next three rooms. As my concentration intensifies and settles into a flow, I don't do much talking. Instead, I mindlessly whistle an earworm between activities; today it's Donny Hathaway's "This Christmas." The next patient is complicated. She's a forty-two-year-old woman crowned by a messy knot of brown locks, in Tweety Bird sweatpants and a half-shirt revealing a belly stretch-marked by childbirth. Her eyes are unfocused through drooping eyelids. She repeatedly moans, "Someone help" while rocking in the chair. The curtain to her room doesn't muffle her laments, and the refrain has been distantly audible for at least fifteen minutes. In the ER, sounds of suffering are a constant soundtrack, and hers was not unusual. We ignored the groans until she was next to be seen.

Now that she's in front of me, I give her my full attention. She never completely opens her eyes or stays consistently engaged for more than a few seconds. In short sentences she tells me that she's short of breath and that her foot is bleeding. From her chart I gleaned that she has diabetes and is on dialysis. "Did you go to dialysis yesterday?"

With her eyes still closed she murmurs, "No."

"What happened?"

"Too cold."

"Doesn't the medicar pick you up?"

"I take the bus." Despite her shoe and sock I can smell the odor of rotting meat coming from her foot. Diabetes is eating her alive. She could end up with an amputation. Evan takes furious notes. I determine what I'll order, file it away in my mind, and then we move on to the next.

This thirty-five-year-old woman with random minor complaints doesn't much register because the last patient was so challenging. It's clear she's worried but well, so I go through the motions. Leaning against the wall since there's no chair, I have my hand on my hip as I ask open questions. I often follow a similar sequence of inquiry so that I can do it while I'm dead tired or distracted. I barely register her answers, but I know Evan will document them clearly. I'm not completely ignoring her, but I'm still processing what medications and labs to order for the previous woman. We wrap up with a "Do you have any questions?" and I move to a sixty-three-year-old man who only speaks Spanish.

I pull the translation tablet into the bay and a live Spanish

translator appears on the screen. This bespectacled man somewhere in the interwebs introduces himself and lets us know we
can start, once in English and again in Spanish. The patient has
thinning gray hair and a clear booming voice. He stands up, lifts
up his brown sweater, and shakes his voluminous belly at the
translation screen. "My belly is full of fluid again. I need it
drained. Even my scrotum is swollen," the translator tells me.
We spend our three minutes discussing why he gets so full of
ascites fluid and what happened last time he came in. I plan orders and the patient asks about his aunt, who's sitting next to
him. She's about eighty, in gray sweats, a black coat, glasses, and
neat silver hair. She also speaks only Spanish and doesn't drive.
They want to know if she can stay with him if he is admitted
overnight, because she has no way to get home. I share that we
can get her a ride home in that case and with that, I step outside
the bay. At my computer, I recall the orders for the woman who
missed dialysis and has the infected foot, then the man with ana-
sarca (the medical term for swelling), and finally the woman
with the vague complaints, in that order.

I've been here an hour now, and the nurses are switching
shifts. I have a lull before they room the next patients, and I notice a dank smell coming from the water/ice dispenser. After
letting Barney from Environmental Services know about it, I
review labs of people who are waiting and scan the track board
to see if that older woman with kidney failure is still in the waiting room. With every bed in the ER occupied, we're now closed
to ambulances. The thirty-six waiting to be seen when I arrived
have grown to forty-three.

I'm interrupted when three family members of an older
woman in the waiting room come to the locked door that leads

to the treatment area. I see the tallest of them, a gray-bearded man wearing a black puffy coat, through the window of the locked door. He summons me with a wave of his hand, and I open the automatic door. I stand on one side of the threshold; they're on the other side. He appears to be in his fifties and is flanked by younger women, who could be his sisters.

"Hey bruh, we've been waiting six hours, my mom is in pain."

"Damn, I'm sorry. Who is your mom? What's her name?"

"Demaris Wilson."

"You right, the wait is way too long. I really apologize for that. Let me see if she can have some Tylenol." One of the younger women sucks her teeth and rolls her eyes. I shake their hands and head back in.

I really don't have much else to offer. Eight years of training, nearing twenty years of experience, and all I have is Tylenol, apologies, and a handshake. And depending on what I find in the chart, maybe not even the Tylenol. A helpless feeling washes over me, and my neck grows hot again. Just as I begin to search for Ms. Wilson's chart a middle-aged woman in a blue soccer jersey walks over from a treatment area asking to see a supervisor.

"I need an IV, I'm in pain, and that man won't give me anything."

While I am a supervisor, I'm not her caregiver. I ask, "Who is your doctor?"

"Tony."

"I'm sorry you're in pain, I want you to feel better. Tony is great, he'll get you what you need." She shakes her head to my bland words, mutters something under her breath, and ambles back to her room. I order Tylenol for Ms. Wilson and search the computer track board—the woman with kidney failure is still in the waiting room.

Now ninety minutes into my shift, I've got three more patients ready to be seen. The first is an eighteen-year-old woman with a silk bonnet covering her hair, gray sweats pulled tight on her legs, and a red T-shirt. She introduces herself as Azalea, enunciating each syllable slowly, carefully, and deliberately. She has a vaginal discharge and says she couldn't be pregnant because she has an IUD. She wants to be checked for everything. This one is straightforward—we screen patients for STIs many times a day. Our service is essential for patients who have few places to go or who appreciate the anonymity of the ED. It's also vital for public health. I'm energized to do something simple, helpful, and preventative—if she finds she has an STI, she's less likely to pass it on. I let her know we'll need blood and urine samples, leave Azalea with a collection cup, and point out the bathroom.

In the next bay is a tall, gangly, eighteen-year-old woman in light blue jeans and a white sweatshirt. Nicole is brown-skinned and has long braids. She is complaining of a sore jaw after being jumped by a group of young women at school. She's calm, but her emotions are as bruised as her face. Her anxious mom is with her and at full attention. I ask about neck pain and loss of consciousness. She doesn't have either and speaks clearly and cogently, allaying my worry about a concussion or broken jaw. Medically this is easy, but the circumstances around it are more complicated. I ask if she'd like to talk to the social worker about school safety. Mom says yes, daughter says no. I let them know they can decide when they're seen in the low-acuity area.

Last of this group is a forty-five-year-old woman with a fever and joint pain. She says the symptoms are consistent with her lupus, and she also has been taking antibiotics for diarrhea. She's wearing a hospital gown, a hospital hat, and hospital socks, all brought from home. Her hair is gray, skin brown, and brow furrowed. She appears many years older than her age. Her story is filled with tangents that emphasize her need for pain medication.

"Doc, can you help me? I need some Dilaudid."

"Yeah, I can help. Tell me, what happened that made today the day to come in?"

"I told you, I'm hurting."

"Got it, I can work on that. But help me understand something: is this the usual pain or a new pain?"

"So many questions! Can't you just give me pain medication?"

Of these three, she's the only clinical conundrum. Either an infection or lupus exacerbation could cause her fever and pain, so we'll evaluate for both. Often people who take narcotics every day experience pain when they haven't had a dose in a while. Is today's pain a sign of illness or narcotic habituation? I can't figure it out in three minutes. I offer her a non-narcotic pain reliever and let her care team in the high-acuity area unravel it when she gets to a room. I retire to the desk to write notes and orders. I'm in a groove and moving quickly.

I'm moving through patients so fast that I'm missing things. While I'm searching the track board to see if the older woman with kidney failure is now being cared for, Frankie, the social worker, finds me. She met Nicole, the young woman who was jumped at school, and asks if I'm worried about her mental state. Honestly, I don't know. I didn't explore the circumstances. I have no idea whether she's being bullied or if she's depressed. I didn't go further. My shoulders slump, and I sigh deeply: I should have queried more. I only gave her three minutes. That wasn't enough.

I am here in my community, in this particular ED, taking care of these specific patients, because at some point I decided this was my mission: to care for my people. To heal our wounds and relieve our suffering. But I can't. I can't get my grandma with kidney failure to a bed, and I can't take my time to investigate the warning signs my little sister shows after being attacked. I know some patients only get one chance to get help, and if we don't seize that opportunity, they miss their shot at relief, safety, freedom, or peace. Here there's more suffering than time or resources. I feel my ears burn red and a flutter in my belly. I can't tell if it's fury, humiliation, or resignation. Now is not the time to dwell; I'll sort it out later. There are more patients to see. I look back to the chart as Frankie walks away, but I know Nicole will visit my thoughts later tonight.

But first I meet this fifty-year-old man. He's smoothly dressed in white huaraches, a white polo shirt, and artfully ripped skinny white jeans. His hair is salt and pepper, his legs are crossed, and he's high as a kite. Aside from having no teeth, he looks much younger than his age.

"I'm here to get checked out so I can go to rehab."

"Rehab? What do you use?"

"Since getting out the pen I get high on embalming fluid." Every day I hear people talk about their coke or heroin habit, occasionally meth, but embalming fluid?! I have to ask more questions.

"Do you drink it?"

"Nah, smoke."

"How do you smoke a liquid?" Laughing, he tells me how they soak tea bags in the fluid and then smoke the leaves. Incredulous, he asks me, "You never heard of this?" But I'm brand-new on smoking embalming fluid. He lets me know he got out of the penitentiary in 2016 and has been on it ever since. "It puts your mind somewhere pleasant," he says. He's happy and charismatic, flirting with the nurse, cracking jokes, asking for a sandwich. His nurse, laughing at the jokes and at my ignorance, clues me in that "embalming fluid" is slang for PCP. But he's not aggressive, like most people on PCP. I direct him to the area where we sober up intoxicated people. Frankie can connect him to rehab there. For just a moment his charm and joy has enchanted the ER. I feel lighter for having met him.

The woman next to him has a grease burn on her right hand. She's a large, brown-skinned woman with a gray hoodie pulled over her head. She's got a plastic bag covering her hand. Her body language is tense, and her words quiver. I ask her about her hand.

"I burned it last month at work."

She went to a different hospital at that time, where they cleaned and dressed it. But she doesn't have insurance and never went to the burn clinic where they referred her for follow-up. Now crying, she tells me, "It hurts, and it smells. I think it's infected." Opening the plastic bag releases a stench that churns my stomach. It's clearly infected, her tendons and bones are visible, and the tissue that hasn't been burned away is swollen. She's unable to move the hand. I take her good hand in both of my hands. "I'm glad you came in. I know this hurts, and I know

you're afraid. We have a lot of work to do to fix this." She begins
to sob—the flow of tears prompts the nurse to find tissue.

"I'm going to call a burn specialist and a hand surgeon. But
first I'll get you pain medications, an X-ray, and labs. Then we're
going to move you to a specialty bed for treatment."

She continues sobbing and avoids eye contact. I wish I had
more time to sit with her, but there are still forty people in the
waiting room. Three minutes.

A lump grows in my throat. I know that this woman is in intense physical pain, but more than that, I know that she's been
suffering for a long time. It's her hand. Not some nagging injury
in a remote part of her body. Her *right* hand. And the smell coming from it is the smell of rot, of death. Coming from the hand
she probably uses to write, to work and dress. She has been feeling it, looking at it, thinking about it. She has likely been on a
carousel of poisonous emotions, panic and shame and grief. I
know it is not just a burn. But the burn is all I have time for. The
lump makes me want to stay, but it also tells me I have to move
on. So I do. Ever onward.

Next to her is a thirty-four-year-old man who says he's suicidal because he has no place to live. He's vague and rambling in
our conversation but I do make out something about the psychiatric medication that he's been taking and his recent discharge
from prison. In a blue Adidas sweat suit and blue shell toes, he's
got a military cut and pudgy, childlike cheeks—he speaks in the
idiom of lockup. His body language comes from prison as well:
no eye contact. I ask the standard questions to gauge risk factors
for completing suicide: He doesn't have a gun but knows where
to get one. He's unemployed and has no idea how to find a job.
He lives on the street without support. I don't know if we can

help, but I'll direct him to the area where psychiatry can see him. And he'll join the others who need help for their depression and suicidal ideation. He calls me "sir" and thanks me for my time.

That was a tough stretch, but I go back to whistling and typing. Rob, one of the young Black techs, approaches me at my desk, an expectant look on his face. He tells me he just finished nursing school. Rob is a nurse! He loves the Bears, is efficient with his work, and is smooth with the patients. Not only does he have good judgment, but he also has depth and warmth. He's going to be a great nurse. He leaves in a month. I dap him.

"When you get your first check, you're going to pass out. Nurse money is long!"

He laughs. "Doc, I got bills, but you know I may have to treat myself," he says.

A commotion around the corner diverts our attention, and we walk over. A patient is shouting at Nurse Roxanne—it's the patient in the blue soccer jersey who wanted pain medication. Roxanne is yelling back when I stroll over, touch her arm, and whisper, "Don't take the bait." Roxanne stops, takes a breath, and disengages by sending the patient back to her room. She's still angry but refocuses. We've all been there.

The next three are up. A robust twenty-three-year-old man who was in a car accident five days earlier and is wearing a T-shirt sized to reveal his gym work. He says everything hurts. An overweight thirty-five-year-old woman in leggings and a sweatshirt is dizzy and weak. She thinks she's pregnant. And last, a thirty-five-year-old French-speaking man. I pull out my rusty French and learn he's suffering from a headache and dizziness. I search my memory for the word for "cough" when his companion reminds me it's *toux*. The patient is lethargic; his companion is energetic. Both are meticulously dressed, with unblemished brown skin. They don't ask where I learned French, and I don't ask where they're from. I'm acting without thinking, one after the next, whistling to fill the silence. I'm a short-order cook flipping burgers at lunch hour.

Before I get to my computer the nurse asks me to look at one more. A twenty-seven-year-old woman came in after being beaten unconscious with a metal pipe by a jealous rival. When I walk into the bay, the woman offers me a crack-toothed smile. Her laugh is punctuated by a smoker's cough, and she's wearing a team sweatshirt.

"Bears fan?"

"Yup. Since I was a kid." We quickly discover that we've both hated every Bears quarterback for the past twenty years. I inspect a jagged wound on the left side of her forehead and work through the dried blood caked in her blond-highlighted hair. She lets me know that she is familiar with the Emergency Department.

"I was here in April when a press at work crushed these four fingers." She holds up her right hand, which has only a thumb remaining. With the gesture for approval permanently on her dominant hand, it doesn't seem like much has gone in her favor. She hasn't yet returned to work and now awaits disability benefits. Her affect is sunny and jovial, but I'm terrified for her. We can fix her face and CT her head, but losing fingers may keep her from work permanently, and disability benefits require a byzantine process that too often provides less money than is needed to live.

By now my shift has become an exercise in endurance. Despite my preparation, I'm hungry, and glimmers of annoyance have grown into a feeling of pins and needles in my head and belly. Many ER doctors develop bad coping habits to relieve these feelings that are hard to quell. Alcoholism, overeating, reckless sex, cocaine—all responses to pressure and stress—are common. The pace of misery never relents. The volume of illness never slackens. The depths of despair never become routine. Day after day. All jobs present a perseverance challenge of one kind or another. And all become mundane. But they all exact a toll. For us the challenge is to avoid becoming inured to suffering or crippled by it. We struggle to maintain our humanity in the face of suffering and our own fatigue. As we persist, our patients teach us about themselves and the world. But only if we listen.

I'm almost halfway done with this eight-hour shift. I step in to see a seventy-three-year-old man who had a stroke a couple of months ago. After his hospital stay for treatment, he was discharged to rehab and is now home. In a wheelchair, he appears well cared for, wearing gray sweatpants with a racing stripe and a gray shirt. His wife is with him in a knit winter hat and a black blazer, prominently, and appropriately, sporting a Superman lapel button. I note the sharp line tracing his meticulous white beard and compare it to my own scraggly, patchy facial hair. While his right arm is puffy and swollen, his nails are manicured and clean. He's clearly loved but is not doing well. He looks around and grimaces on occasion but is otherwise quiet and slumped. His wife brought him in because he's regressing. He isn't moving his right side, he is not speaking anymore, he's disoriented and getting weaker. I ask her about her goals for him and between the lines of the conversation we implicitly acknowledge that he's never going to recover fully. She says, "I want him home, walking with a limp and talking with a slur." I look at his paralyzed leg and see his mortality. I think of my father's stroll through life, getting older and grayer every year. Of my own hip that is growing achy like the hinge of a screen door, rusting and squeaking more loudly every year. Of our collective march toward death. This man is closer than most but being loved every step of the way. I'm not sure how much we can do about his deterioration, but we can do something. I engage Frankie for social work resources, order lab tests, and launch him to the care team in the main ER.

The next sequence of three are a thirty-nine-year-old woman with fuzzy boots and a tattoo of red lips on her right forearm. She's here for chest pain and palpitations. A sixty-seven-year-old man who missed two days of dialysis. He's in plaid pants and a plaid shirt—but two different plaids. Finally, a twenty-four-year-old woman who is curled in a ball in the chair. She has had vaginal bleeding for two weeks. She starts our engagement by saying she was seen somewhere else for this and was treated like a dog. This jars me out of my rhythm. At this point in the shift my patients aren't just blurring together; I'm starting to look at each as an embodied medical problem and not a person.

Each of these three has a real health issue and specific needs we can meet. For the woman with chest pain we have an EKG, a chest X-ray, and labs. For the man who missed dialysis we have labs and emergency dialysis if necessary, and for the woman with pelvic pain and bleeding we have an exam and ultrasound. My training and experience let me execute without thinking, filling the space with Christmas carols. Sometimes that mechanized execution is helpful, but not always. I shudder to think that there is a patient out there who is telling another doctor that I "treated her like a dog." Still, I dispatch these cases and move on.

Next three are a twenty-nine-year-old man with immaculately groomed locks and bloody diarrhea. He recently received penicillin for syphilis, and now the week of diarrhea has sapped his strength. A twenty-four-year-old woman shows me her right eye, which is pink and crusted. The third is a twenty-three-year-old man with a throbbing abscess on his left forearm from injecting drugs. His T-shirt is dirty and stretched, and his baggy jeans have rips that were not planned by any fashion designer. With matted hair and an angelic smile, he's the only white patient I've seen this shift. His straight teeth, use of the King's English, and academic tone let me know he comes from a family with money that valued education.

"This arm is tender and throbs."

"Has this happened before?"

"I've been injecting drugs since I was fourteen, I've had these abscesses every few years. Rehab has helped, but I'm using again."

I've seen these abscesses many times, sometimes with broken needles still in the tissue. I order an X-ray of the arm to ensure there is no metal inside.

These last three straightforward problems are perfect for a local clinic. I proceed with precision and focus, three minutes each. For some, efficiency leads to relief, and others feel resentment—they all want to tell their story. And each will be surprised when they get the bill. The complaints don't slow me. I pace through them but can't help a cringe of shame. These people have waited hours to see me. People queue as though they're waiting to meet an oracle, and then we disappoint them with the banality of the process. I wonder if to them I'm no different than the fraudulent wizard Dorothy finds in Oz.

I'm back at my computer workstation talking with Rob about what he's going to buy with his first nursing check when we're interrupted by an old man. He's in his socks wandering around the ED pleasantly drunk and talking to anyone who will listen. His plaid work shirt is unbuttoned, exposing his chest. His black pants are unbuckled and sagging. Emily the nurse walks up to him and laughs.

"Sir, where are you supposed to be?"

"I'm right here!" he slurs.

I laugh too as she escorts him back to his room nodding greetings to everyone on his way. That's my cue to indulge for a minute and grab a coffee and a Rice Krispies treat from the patient care stash.

With almost four hours done and four to go, I stroll to the break room. One of the security guards is in there sipping coffee, still wearing his winter hat and coat. We silently give each other the nod Black men give to each other. He's got the TV tuned to BET. I finish my Rice Krispies treat and wash an apple while I keep an eye on Martin Payne talking smack to his best friend, Tommy. With a satisfying crunch and juicy tartness, the apple numbs the pins and needles in my stomach. I hope the older woman with kidney failure has gotten a room, but I gain nothing by trying to find out. I give the guard the nod as I head back to the fray.

5

Dear Nicole,

I examined your face after you were jumped at school. Your mom was terrified for your safety—you seemed annoyed. You waited for hours, and then I didn't spend nearly enough time with you, only enough to check out your injuries and then the social worker came to talk with you. I regret that I couldn't do more, and I'm sorry. It all happened so slow—and then so fast: languishing in the waiting room and then a procession of people in scrubs who barely introduce themselves, each talking to you for five minutes before they disappear. This may have been your first visit to the ER, but I'm here every week, every month, every year. Unfortunately, none of this is unique to our ER; these circumstances exist in almost every ER in every big city. I wish I could have spent more time with you, learning more about the circumstances of your injury and addressing more than the wounds I can see. I was rushing then, but I want to tell you about the ER, why you waited, and why I was so brief with you.

People come to the ER for a lot of different reasons. Some people need help with the life-altering health events like strokes and shootings, and others are looking for care of everyday problems. You probably gathered this while you lingered in the waiting room. We serve an unfiltered cross section of our otherwise stratified society without division. Even on the segregated South Side, we serve Black and white people, executives and laborers, young and old, men and women, people with plans for the future and those who know the end is near. The Emergency Department is one of the few places where our whole community converges. Then, once the patient gets a treatment room, the trappings of culture and status are stripped away, and all that remains is a common experience: illness and injury shape each of our lives. But if our human frailty brings us all together, our specific pain and its possibility of relief can be very different.

At eighteen this might be your first visit to the ER, but it's not likely your last—everyone visits the ER at some point. Patients who come to us are not just a random assortment of injuries and illnesses. Instead, the ailments we treat uncover quirks in our society: like the way violence peaks on humid summer nights and how alcohol is involved in so many car collisions. The thousands who come to us every year reflect a society that stratifies and ranks. By law we are charged to care for all who come, no matter what. But even here, some patients receive rationed care while others obtain the finest services available in the world. You waited for hours and then received minutes of my time, but there are people who use back doors and work-arounds to get prompt care and fast test results, and their doctors take the time to hear their entire story. These patterns reveal public health dilemmas and our collective failure to take care of each other. Still: it is the most practical and indispensable facility in the American health-care system, where lives begin and end.

For much of its history, the Emergency Department didn't provide high-quality care. In the early twentieth century EDs were under-staffed, dangerous places where doctors started and finished their careers—places that people generally avoided except in, well, an emergency. In those days, when people fell ill, they'd call their doctor. For a child with a fever, a conversation with a doctor was often enough to settle the matter. Lacerations meant the physician would make a house call, with stitches given at the kitchen table. But when the problem was more serious, like a broken limb or chest pain, people would meet their clinician in the Emergency Department, day or night. On arrival, their general practitioner would assess the issue, and if they couldn't handle it, they'd consult colleagues to take out an ap-pendix or set a bone. To make this system of personalized emergency care work, patients needed to have doctors, and those doctors had to be always available to their patients, any time of day. But of course, that is impossible.

Nicole, do you have a doctor? Would you have called them before you came in? If you did call, did they call you back? This quandary, if it is yours, is the same faced by people before modern EDs: lots of people didn't have a doctor to call, and when they did, their physi-cians were often busy. With full clinic days and hospitalized patients requiring their attention, doctors were often unable to meet their sick and injured patients in the ED. When that happened, folks showed up in EDs seeking care from anyone who could help. Just like you did. While a lot of things have changed, some things stay the same.

At that time, doctors in training filled the gap. On their way to inde-pendent practice, physicians rotated through or moonlighted in emer-gency departments. When my dad was a resident, he picked up moonlighting shifts in the ER to bring home extra money. Specialists and generalists would also attend to unaffiliated patients who arrived in the Emergency Department. They were untrained for all the emergencies that might present on any given day, and matching the right doctors to the right patients cost precious time. Sometimes this came at the expense of limbs—and lives. My father recalls being overmatched by the breadth of illnesses that he had to manage. The system needed doctors who understood all kinds of emergencies, who knew that headaches could mean anxiety, stroke, *or* carbon monoxide poisoning and who could also set broken bones and treat depression.

Changing social structures in the '60s and '70s, before you and I were even born, introduced emergency medicine as a specialty. Breaking medical traditions, in 1961 a handful of doctors abandoned their general practice and chose to take care of people in emergency departments, committed themselves to attending to the ED day and night. By 1965 Medicare and Medicaid provided payment for these services, and one year later the Highway Safety Act set standards for ambulance transports to emergency departments. Eight doctors in Michigan created what is now the American College of Emergency Physicians in 1968. By the end of the 1970s emergency medicine was incorporated in the American Board of Medical Specialties, certifying it as a nationally recognized field of medicine. This laid the foundation for the profession I chose.

It took a while before this specialty became widespread, but now almost all the doctors you see in the ER are specialists in emergency medicine. In my first job after being trained in what's now known as "EM," I worked in a hospital where few of the other doctors had similar training. While they benefited from decades of experience, the broad array of emergencies that bring people to the hospital often strained their abilities. One day, a colleague faced a four-year-old boy who would not flex his elbow. It started after his dad lifted him up by his wrists to playfully swing him. Despite negative X-rays and Tylenol, the youngster kept favoring that arm, and my colleague couldn't make sense of it. My training taught me this was a classic presentation of nursemaid's elbow—this means that a ligament in his elbow is misaligned. I performed a quick maneuver to fix the child's elbow, and my colleague never missed that diagnosis again. As more EM-trained doctors joined the hospital, the quality of care gradually changed for the better.

Steadily emergency departments everywhere began to reflect the needs of their patients—here you can get a COVID vaccine or get help when you're feeling depressed. ERs now have features of a surgical suite, a psychiatric ward, and a public aid office. There are rooms with leaded walls for X-rays of limbs and CT scans to identify the inner workings of brains and organs. Bedside ultrasound machines diagnose internal bleeding in unstable patients and guide invasive procedures. Laboratory results return in minutes and hours rather than days so that we can act on the information immediately. Pharmacists mix drugs on the spot to quickly raise or lower blood pressure, thin or clot blood, arouse or sedate patients. There are rooms to isolate those who are infected and to protect patients who are suicidal or violent. Social workers assist those who need help at home and others who need to get away from abuse. From administrative resources to equipment, there are policies to help us manage any emergency twenty-four hours a day. After forty years of refining, the American College of Emergency Physicians outlines core ED services over a span of thirteen dense pages.

As the field has matured, emergency medicine physicians like me deploy all these capabilities so that they can treat you and all of the other patients who arrive at the ER. Perceived to be jacks of all trades and masters of none, we do know one thing very well: how to recognize and manage life threats. While some specialties, like cardiology, focus on an organ and others, like pediatrics, on a life phase, emergency medicine is focused on identifying and managing serious illness. This means distinguishing chest pain caused by heart attacks from indigestion, anxiety, or pneumonia and understanding how to treat each of those ailments.

Training to acquire those special skills spans a three- or four-year residency after medical school. With long days and intense work, residency is structured to build an array of skills: stabilizing critical patients, applying diagnostics, weighing data, aptitude with pharmaceutical remedies, dexterity with airway and pain management. We deploy advanced technology and drugs that touch deep inside bodies with a precision that can seem like magic. We also look for social issues that lead to disease—I'm of the generation of doctors who came into the field to marry the treatment of physical, social, and societal emergencies. As I learned to identify patterns of hunger and homelessness, I've been frustrated by how few treatments we have to address these underlying issues. While medicine pushes the leading edge of twenty-first-century know-how, social services dawdle in the nineteenth. This training is why I know that getting jumped at school, the way you were, isn't just a matter of treating the physical injury. We can also screen for bullying and help you with interventions. But that day I didn't take the time to dig into the second layer, beyond the injury, because I was distracted by the legions of people in the waiting room. I'm sorry.

Emergency medicine doctors like me learn to make high-stakes decisions with incomplete information and lives on the line, repeatedly, professionally, and hopefully with empathy. I didn't get to ask about your assault because much of my job is to detect the most dangerous disorders even if it requires a significant amount of time and energy. Occasionally someone who just has indigestion will be admitted to the hospital out of an abundance of caution. Other times, a person having a heart attack will be sent home out of rushed error. I must balance those extremes, and when so much is at stake, errors are costly one way or the other. When things are busy, which is all the time, I often don't have time to learn about backstories, but I try to make sure someone else does. Those doctors who prioritize, learn to be calm under pressure, have good people skills, lead teams well, and enjoy working with their hands are the best in the specialty. Once I saw that you were okay, my thoughts turned to the potential disasters in the other rooms, arriving by ambulance or in the waiting room. That is not an excuse. It is just a reason.

While we're always ready for the worst cases, is that who actually comes in? You noticed while in the waiting room that few people looked like they were about to keel over. And I bet you also saw regular people with regular problems. And you're mostly right. The National Hospital Ambulatory Medical Care Survey, which is performed every year, in 2017 analyzed 140 million visits to EDs around the country, spanning all ages and diseases. Only about 1 percent of ED visits required immediate resuscitation and another 10 percent were emergencies that could not wait. These are the people whose lives hang in the balance. Approximately 34 percent of visits were people who needed urgent assistance but could wait up to an hour. The data shows us an ED patient population that is about evenly divided between problems that are so severe they cannot wait even an hour longer to receive care and people with nagging issues that can be managed without as much time pressure. This mix will vary depending on the season, population, and location. In our ER we see a lot of very sick people and many of them wait a long time, but it's the folks with minor problems who wait the longest, filling up the waiting room.

In neighborhoods like ours on the South Side, Black people and poor people disproportionately use the Emergency Department. In 2017, 25 percent of Black folks had at least one ED visit, even though they comprised only 13 percent of the population. In comparison, 18 percent of white people used the ED. Regardless of race, 30 percent of people who fall under the poverty line had at least one ER visit in 2017, compared to 13 percent of those who make more than four times the poverty limit. Not surprisingly, poor Black people were the highest ED users of all. Thirty-three percent of Black people in poverty used the ED once, and 18 percent came twice or more. This data is reflected in our waiting room, bursting with lower-income Black folks seeking care for both minor ailments and health catastrophes.

Television shows about ERs make you think it's all romance and drama, but what we do is mostly mundane. When someone like you arrives looking for help, they check in with the triage nurse, who assesses the patient's vital signs and gathers personal information and family history to determine the urgency of the situation. The triage nurse then assigns an Emergency Severity Index score. A score between one and five is derived from that data and stratifies people by the gravity of the issue and likely resource requirements. This standard triage occurs in almost every ER in the country. Level 1 patients require immediate life-saving intervention: they have stopped breathing or face impending death and are rushed in to be resuscitated. Level 5 patients are stable, with normal vital signs and problems like ankle sprains or sore throats—they can safely wait hours before their condition changes. Everyone else falls in between. Patients whom the triage nurse deems Level 1 or 2 are supposed to be moved to a treatment area almost immediately. The rest return to the waiting room. This same ordering process takes place for patients who arrive by ambulance. While en route, paramedics call in the patient's vital signs and history so the ED can calculate the person's severity and assess whether they need immediate resuscitation or can wait. You were given a Level 4 score.

This Emergency Severity Index orders a crucial decision: which patients need care first and who can wait. While you'd expect this determination to hinge on which patient has the most critical medical problem, in fact the ESI is weighted to predict who will need the most resources. There are other variables as well. Multiple studies have shown that bias in the algorithm leads it to do a poor job of predicting the severity of Black people's medical needs, at times underestimating their illness and other times saying they're sicker than they are. If you were raised like I was, you won't be surprised to learn that bias is baked into everything, but it's still jarring to see it where we least expect it.

Once patients get through triage, people have different experiences depending on the hospital. Some EDs are structured to take care of everybody almost immediately, but in others the next step for most people is a long wait. Once in a treatment area, a patient meets a team of professionals. This is where I met you and where you met my squad. Physicians, nurses, techs, transporters, and security and cleaning staff all collaborate to care for people. I'm the attending physician, and while everyone has their own roles, the responsibility is ultimately mine. The treatment areas are where patients are examined and have their blood drawn, X-rays shot, and laboratory tests processed, and all the while the department remains safe and clean. We follow a process of elimination to search for and treat emergencies until threats are solved or ruled out. While most people go home feeling better, others don't go home; they're admitted overnight, requiring surgery or intensive care to solve problems that we've found and begun treating in the ED. As you experienced, diagnosis and intervention can take hours, include a lot of people, and cost thousands of dollars.

We work right where the community and the hospital connect. We sort through and treat hundreds of people a day. Overcrowded with sick folks and others who have basic needs, our job is in an unsorted, unpredictable, and sometimes risky venue. Patients are often deliri-ous, intoxicated, psychotic, and at their wit's end. While you waited you probably smelled alcohol and witnessed conflict. We're on guard when people yell and become confrontational because it's routine for patients to throw blood, heave chairs, swing fists, and shoot guns at EM doctors and staff. In a 2018 survey of emergency medicine doc-tors, 47 percent reported being physically assaulted at work. We work closely with security. We couldn't function without them.

Beyond physical violence, emergency medicine physicians like me confront losing our faith. Student loan debt, a commitment to healing, administrative pressure, and hopes for professional freedom create competing goals that cannot be reconciled. Doctors like me are often pushed into unbearable struggles with moral and ethical dilemmas that flow from administrative and financial realities that demand con-cessions in our values. When five people in the waiting room deterio-rate with critical illness but we have only two beds available, who goes first? How about when we face these choices every day, week after week, year after year? Like soldiers who are forced to kill in ethically ambiguous settings, we face conflicts in principle that are impossible to resolve. These moral injuries lead to depression and anxiety.

I wanted to talk to you more, to understand the circumstances of your assault, assess if you're safe, but extra time with you would have taken me away from a waiting room full of sick people. I can't do it all. I felt like a failure, and I'm not alone; many of my peers feel this too.

There is a high rate of burnout for ER doctors that has accelerated now that we've seen so many of our peers fall to COVID. Most hospitals combat burnout with therapy referrals, guided meditation, and occasionally free food, but the root of the conflict is much deeper. Years of training empowers ER physicians with incredible skills, but the psychological toll of the work hobbles many of us. Others become hardened to the human crisis we oversee daily.

Beyond that, I know you waited forever, and that's not an accident. All of these things happen within a system. The question is: why is the system designed like this?

We strive to care for people in a sequence based on the severity of their disease. But in the past, even the sickest patients were sent away if they were unable to pay. The Emergency Medical Treatment and Active Labor Act, known as EMTALA, was passed in 1986 to end this practice. The law says hospitals that take Medicare and have emergency departments must screen and treat patients with emergency medical conditions regardless of their ability to pay, insurance status, citizenship, or race. After years of EDs sending poor and undesirable patients away to public hospitals or to suffer on their own, Ronald Reagan signed into law a mandate to do more. However, this policy was not funded.

As a result, the law pushed hospitals to find other ways to fill their beds with paying patients and to avoid the poor people who fill their ED waiting rooms. Rather than improving access to emergency care, EMTALA's impact was more complicated.

Many hospitals closed their emergency departments and trauma centers due to the financial pressure of caring for poor and uninsured patients. Other hospitals undertook administrative policies that slowed care in the emergency departments to a crawl. When things are busy, many hospitals fill their beds and then hold admitted ED patients in the emergency department rather than bringing them up to the wards. When the hospital is declared "full," ED patients who need inpatient care are "boarded" in ED exam rooms or hallways until a bed is available. Critically ill ED patients often wait the longest for admission because ICU beds are particularly valuable and in short supply. An ED full of boarded patients ties up space, equipment, and personnel that would otherwise be available to serve incoming (paying) patients.

The long wait time and teeming waiting room you experienced came about because our hospital was full. The unquenchable health needs of poor and Black folks in communities where there aren't many health-care outlets drive them disproportionately to the ED, but that doesn't tell the entire story. Being "full" is shaped by administrative decisions. While admitted ER patients board for hours— sometimes days—elective surgical procedures and transferred patients compete to access that scarce hospital space. In neighborhoods like ours, where hospitals have to meet tremendous demand for care, many hospitals maintain special pathways for high-paying patients at the expense of the unfiltered (and often low-paying) patients who visit the ER. In this way they meet their legal mandate to care for everyone regardless of their ability to pay and also resolve their financial bottom line. For hospitals that serve poor and Black patients like this one, the overflowing ER waiting room and lengthy boarding times are acceptable in order to balance their books with paying elective procedures and transfers. Meanwhile, hospitals that are financially flush because they serve wealthier populations are more likely to have ERs that flow swiftly. While you will always wait behind more seriously ill people, had you gone to an ER in the north suburbs, even one that has just as many daily patient visits, it's possible you would have been seen immediately.

Waiting for so long must have felt disrespectful to you, Nicole. The problem is not that long waits create an inconvenience but that they can cost lives. According to a 2012 study, patients who were admitted on days with high ED crowding experienced 5 percent greater odds of death, resulting in three hundred deaths a year. When crowding reaches these dangerous levels, hospitals often reduce inflow by diverting inbound ambulances to other facilities. One facility deciding to divert ambulances fills nearby hospitals and prompts others to follow suit. When that happens, parts of cities experience the health-care equivalent of a rolling blackout. Everyone in that community is affected by the prolonged ambulance transport times, long waits, and disrupted patterns of care. These systemic issues of high demand and manufactured bottlenecks create dangerous conditions in EDs that serve low-income and Black communities like ours all across the country.

Nicole, I've tried to explain at least a part of the system we're all working in, the necessity of triage, the pain that flows through a system balancing capitalism and care, the pain that afflicts patients but also the doctors who try to serve them. I also know that none of that changes what happened to you that day. I hope you understand why I didn't spend enough time with you and why you waited. I don't know what it's worth, but I wanted to take more time, to get to know you, to fix more than your face. I also want you to know this is bigger than me and you; we're both in a system that works against us connecting. I know you felt frustrated—I did too! I worried about you for days. I hope you're okay.

Onward,

tlf

6

MAY 2020

LAST NIGHT I HEARD screams in my dream. I was walking across a pasture toward a picnic where my family was eating. The meadow was not in Chicago but out of a storybook. Green grass to the horizon, spotted with white flowers. A shining sun, beaming but not hot. Unlike when walking in Chicago's parks, I never felt compelled to look down to avoid stepping in dogshit. I could see my parents and sisters on the red checkerboard blanket across the pitch, laughing and having a great time. I was on my way, excited to join, but every few steps I heard the screams. Every time, a woman's terrified yell stopped me in my tracks. It came softly from behind me, loudly from above, with distortion from the left. I'd look to see where it originated, but there was nothing around but green grass and my oblivious family across the field. Over and over I'd resume walking until I was again halted by the scream. I never made it to the picnic.

Over coffee this morning I realize that the scream was from

the Emergency Department. Two nights ago, I was caring for a car accident victim when they rolled in a twenty-three-year-old woman wearing a blood-spattered yellow track suit with gauze covering her face and arms. She had been in a car that was sieved by bullets. One side of her face was made up with lipstick and those false lashes that look like a daddy longlegs, the other side was mashed to currant jelly. Both hands and arms had been shot as well. She must have seen her assailant coming, put up her hands, and caught slugs. Her incoherent mumbling ended when they moved the gauze that covered where her left eye should be. Her scream filled the room, loud enough to be heard over the monitor alarms and physician orders. That was the scream from my dream.

Nowadays my sleep is rarely peaceful. Violence is rampant even as COVID has emptied the streets, closed restaurants, and canceled travel. Social distancing has reshaped Chicago and my life. When I'm not in the ED, I text and Zoom with friends, write, exercise, and take walks with my sister and niece to manage loneliness and fear. Yesterday was a stunning, 70-degree spring day. I walked a couple miles north and west past the ball fields and public pool at Eckhart Park and checked out the huge refurbished playground. With two different kinds of swings and a climbing gym, it's a kids' nirvana. Surrounded by a field of dandelions and shade trees that were starting to bear leaves, it was chained closed. Not a single kid: no laughing, no chasing. It was empty. I spent half that day walking until I couldn't hear the scream anymore, but it returned in my dream anyway.

After processing the nightmare over coffee, I got into an argument with Monroe, my partner. This time of painful isolation has us both on edge. We're long-distance, so we rarely get to see each other in person, and this morning she picked at me for arriving five minutes late to our scheduled FaceTime session. I didn't have the patience to be my best self. Rather than recognize that her response came from a place of loneliness or see that she was pleading for care, I escalated. I demanded understanding and an apology when I knew that would only create more distance. "This isn't fair. I need you to apologize," is the last thing I said before we parted. I know we need to be kinder to each other to get through this, and I know that this morning, I haven't been kind. I start to calm down and prepare for work. In the shower I plan my apology. I don blue scrubs, blue and pink argyle socks, and a gray cloth mask fresh out of the dryer. My bag holds snacks and a bottle of water. This apology is going to be tough because I can't shake the idea that I'm not wrong. Even though I know that doesn't matter.

The bucket boy is back. He's at the Garfield Boulevard off-ramp, drumming solos with his mask under his chin. I pull up to the light listening to a dance track whose few decipherable words include the phrase "I am now and now is me." He seems to hear my music and syncs up with the beat. He deserves more than the couple bucks I offer him. Two months ago, I accepted that I'll probably be infected, but now I feel defiant. I will not capitulate. This is what I trained for, and I intend to execute for as long as I can.

As I near the hospital I see that Washington Park is still abandoned. A few older Black men walk toward the corner of Michigan Avenue and Garfield. The man who pushes himself around in a wheelchair is still gone, as is his diminutive friend. I wonder what has happened to them.

I'm taking over this shift from Laird. A generation older than

me, he was one of the doctors who taught me emergency medicine. After changing into hospital scrubs, a disposable mask,
head cover and eye protection, I greet him to take over his patients. In-person human contact is the best part of my shifts, so
I'm excited to talk with him. Laird confides that his new COVID
routines threw him for a loop today. "Sheesh," he says. "I have
to tell you, I'm glad you're here. I've had a bizarre day."

"Tough one?"

"Getting out of the house is so complicated now. I misread
my shift time and arrived an hour and a half late." He's masked
up, in hospital scrubs and dress shoes, and seems overjoyed to
just vent.

Now two months into the pandemic, the initial convulsion
has given way to new patterns. Laird and I speak across a desk
rather than side by side. Our facial expressions hidden by masks,
we try to discern everything we can from tone of voice, from
eyes. Laughs are louder now, hand gestures more definitive.
Every other desk monitor is now turned off and blocked by a
sign indicating the space is not in use to meet the required physical distance. Before we begin signing out patients, I embark on
an elaborate sequence of disinfecting my chair, keyboard, and
mouse. This may or may not make any difference for my safety,
but the choreographed ritual is reassuring and signals to others
that I'm serious. As I clean, Laird dances back and forth as he
speaks, moving away from me when he realizes he's talking too
close and then moving back toward me when he's gotten so far
away that I strain to hear him over the din of the ER.

One of the patients he transitions to my care is a thirty-two-
year-old woman.

"The young woman in Bed 18 came in by ambulance. She

was having a normal day, all of a sudden she fell to the ground and couldn't get up."

I stop cleaning to hear this. "What?"

"Yeah, she's young. On arrival she couldn't move her left side, not even grasp with her left hand. It recovered a little, but not much. Anyway, she's getting directed thrombolytics right now." He pauses thoughtfully. "Have you seen anything like this?"

"Umm, no, never." I'm listening closely. Young people who suffer devastating strokes are very rare.

"A couple hours later, her test came back positive for COVID. This is the first stroke I've seen associated with the virus."

I just shake my head. What is there to say? She was infected, and her first and only symptom was the stroke. Until she returns from the radiology suite where her stroke is being treated, we won't know how she's doing. None of us have seen anything like this. The coronavirus is making us relearn medicine.

Social distancing orders and fear of COVID have kept people away from the Emergency Department. Our patient volume has fallen by half. Now the waiting room is empty. Patients who would've waited hours or more for an inpatient bed now go upstairs within minutes. Consultants who dragged their feet before seeing our patients are suddenly prompt. After the initial COVID surge, fewer colleagues have fallen ill with coronavirus and the look of fear and the hushed tones are gone. ER conversations have moved from what we're doing to stay safe to how we're staying sane while shut in at home. Previously I turned off my emotions as best I could and pushed through shifts, trying to return to normal life outside the hospital as quickly as possible. Now, there is no normal life outside, so I linger in the comfort of the ER's familiar pace and people. A few days earlier, a beloved peer, in her goldfish-ornamented hair cover and matching yellow goggles, noted how the hospital's COVID focus has created ER efficiency.

"Look at these wait times. It's like a normal emergency department!"

"Right? This must be what it's like to work in a community hospital with an efficient ER," I replied. "We need things to go this way from now on. But if they did, we'd never make any money."

"Okay, but are we in the business of making money or the practice of saving lives?" We both laughed loudly and got back to work.

My first patient is a fifty-four-year-old man still groggy from a heroin overdose. He was found unresponsive in a car where he snorted a dime bag with his friend. When he would not wake up, his companion called 911. Paramedics arrived and injected him with naloxone, and he came around. He sports a crispy haircut, which is unusual in these times of social distance, and his heavy eyelids pause with each blink. I stand in the room, masked, along with a masked resident who's leading the conversation into the circumstances of his illness. After a couple of minutes of conversation, she asks, "Did you use drugs?" He pauses and after a side-eye responds that he snorted heroin. I jump in. "When was the last time you used before today?"

He's now defensive. "Why?"

"Usually, people who use every day don't get knocked out, so you must not use often." I soften my tone, hoping he'll open up. His body visibly untenses.

"Oh yeah, you're right. The last time was five months ago."

Five months sounds like a bid. I ask if he had been locked up, and he confirms.

"Welcome home, fam."

He grins and thanks me. Then he explains that he was released early only because of COVID.

The resident and I sit down and debrief. Narcotic overdoses have become common again. The proliferation of fentanyl boosts street heroin's potency, and COVID has led to early release for people who have lost their tolerance. We regularly care for older folks who have used heroin for years but are now overdosing. This patient's care is easy, we just observe him to make sure he continues to recover, but we can't forget to counsel him—or to send him home with a prescription for naloxone so someone can save him if this happens again when the paramedics are too far away.

I stroll to Room 10 to meet a twenty-nine-year-old man with a headache. It's unusual for an Asian man to come to our ED, so right away I assume he's affiliated with the university. He's sitting in a chair with the lights off, holding his head. Code-switching to a collegial tone, I say, "Hello, sir. I'm Dr. Fisher." He responds in kind: "I'm Andrew. Nice to meet you." He sits up straight, makes direct eye contact. We exchange elbow bumps.

"I understand you're having a headache? Tell me about it."

"Well, it's a long story, but last night I was on call and began to experience occipital throbbing. I thought I might be sleep-deprived, but after resting today I awoke with worsening pain in the same location. I felt it's best to come in." He's poised and direct and provides descriptions in the same order that we use when writing our medical histories. I probe further.

"You were on call?"

It turns out he's a third-year resident doctor in internal medicine. Ten years ago, while an undergrad in Boston, he had brain surgery to fix an aneurysm. For him, headaches aren't simple. I approach health discussions with medical professionals differently: more specific questions and more medical terms.

"Do you have diplopia?"

"No."

"Photophobia?"

"No, but I had a scotoma in my right visual field when it started, and now my left arm is heavy."

While this could be a migraine, I'd hate to miss another aneurysm, and so we engage a neurologist and order a CT scan of Andrew's brain. We discuss his treatment and diagnostic plan. He works here too, so he understands that he'll be here all day.

I return to my computer and begin to compose an apology text to Monroe. I need to tell her that while she's never expressed them to me out loud, I understand her feelings of abandonment and uncertainty. Being unable to talk in person, eat together, and laugh makes everything harder and more complicated. I'll let her know I understand the impulse to fill in what's missing with our imagination. We're both lonely, and arguing over small things only leaves us lonelier. Doing this by text while at work in the ED is not great, but letting it linger wastes time neither of us have.

As I start to write, I notice our rotating intern has stepped away to eat. Twenty years ago, when I was an intern, there was no such thing as "away eating." We didn't eat on shift unless we brought food and wolfed it down while hiding in the telemetry radio room. My headache patient who's a resident let me know that he got four hours of sleep on ICU call. When I was on call in the intensive care unit as a resident, I rarely saw the bunk beds in the call room and only went to those private quarters to brush my teeth before rounds in the morning. We spent all night on our feet, remaining at the hospital from 6 in the morning until 6 P.M. the next day—thirty-six hours. We did this every third night. Four uninterrupted hours of sleep was unheard of.

Back then, lip service was given to self-care, but that generally went no further than drinking water and using the bathroom so that we could get back to work. I trained in abusive and inhumane times, when residency was as much a test of resilience and endurance as clinical training. Work-hour restrictions implemented halfway through my residency were haphazardly implemented. A couple of my peers got divorced during residency, and we all had varying levels of depression and resignation. Residents today still suffer, but it's much better. I jest with the residents, telling them how hard it used to be *back in my day*. It's in fun, but I'm still scarred by the wounds residency inflicted on my younger self. I wouldn't wish it on anyone.

Right on cue, my resident Theresa complains about being house staff. The electronic medical record takes so much of her shift that she never gets to spend time with her patients. She works so much that she can't see her wife. The painful start to a career that will be marked by sacrifice. This is not the time to compare suffering, so we discuss how to manage this expense over a lifetime. We discuss coping, remaining present, and balance. I want to reveal it all, the lifetime of struggle ahead of her, but there's a patient to see. I let her think and write notes on the computer while I go see him on my own.

This skater named Morris hit his head when he fell on a

half-pipe yesterday. Morris is a tall man, twenty-four years old, with fuzzy cornrows under a patterned cap, wearing matching T-shirt and shorts. He is slumped in the reclining chair with his hand in his shorts and a COVID mask below his nose. I introduce myself and ask him to raise his mask over his nose, for his protection and mine. Morris barely makes eye contact, shifts his mask with one hand while the other remains in his shorts.

A sharp tone frames his words: "Can I get a room with a bed? My head hurts."

He's annoyed—angry about the wait, the chair, the fall, and the mask. All reasonable. While he wasn't knocked out and doesn't have signs of bleeding, he's probably got a concussion but is otherwise fine. He's not reassured by our conversation and wants more, so I offer him a head CT to be sure. He doesn't know if he wants it.

"I waited for hours, now it's on me to decide?"

"No worries, bruh," I tell him, "it's not on you. Let me get you some Tylenol, and let's do the scan." He agrees but his fist remains tightly curled.

I'm in the ED all the time, but for my patients their ED visit is a special day. Most people rarely come to the ED, and when they do, it's with an expectation that their sense of emergency will be precisely matched by the hospital staff—it's what they've seen in a hundred movies and television shows. When they confront bureaucratic waits, unexpected treatment paths, unsympathetic registration, and inefficient care, they're incensed. Anger is common. Yelling is common. Even violence—I've seen doctors punched in the face.

People with power and agency call their doctor or their influential friends to pull whatever strings they can to ensure they never face these rusty gears. Everyone else suffers longer than they should and is ignored when they demand more. I can neither fix the system in the middle of a shift nor work around the obstacles for every person every time. After being forced by rules or resource limitations to deny patients simple graces like pillows or a visitor, I used to avoid returning to their rooms out of shame. I'd close the door and try to forget. No matter what I said, they interpreted my inability to deliver as mistreatment. And while my avoidance protected me from feeling like a failure, it added to their perception of institutional neglect. They're right. Their anger and sadness are justified, and their assessment of my role is accurate. I am a perpetuator of the system's mistreatment, and I am also a casualty, trying to do the best I can with what I have.

On my way back to my desk to complete the skater's chart, I'm drawn in by a nurse and a tech jovially discussing their search for a baller.

"Dr. Fisher, do you know the Viagra Triangle?"

"Uhhhhh, yeah?"

"C'mon, Doc. Put us on. How do we get there? We're trying to get saved."

We're all laughing at this get-rich-quick scheme.

"It's over on Rush Street between Chicago and Division," I explain. That's the city's best spot for watching the courtship between the aspirational and the acquisitive. I joke with them that I also want to get saved from the everyday grind, when I remember that I still haven't sent that text to my partner. After all that prep and rumination, I dash off a few words about being sorry and how we need to talk more that evening. Looking down fifteen minutes later, I can see that she's responded, but I will read it later.

The woman in Room 19 is here because she cannot urinate. She's fifty-one years old, in a cloth mask, a head wrap, and clear lunch-lady gloves. Sitting in the chair farthest from the door and away from the bed, she makes eye contact with me.

"Hello, Ms. Franklin, what's wrong?"

She begins a long, meandering story about her regional pain syndrome that she refers to with an acronym, CRPS, that I've never heard before. She tells me about her nerve stimulation implants for pain, a hip replacement, and kidney stones. Her lupus caused blood clots in her legs and lungs. I think about how I feel when I'm rushing to find a bathroom and compare it to her comfortable countenance and winding story. If she's not stressed, I'm not stressed, so I sit on the bed next to her unused gown and listen. Finally she gets to why she's here.

"I can't urinate, it comes only in dribbles."

"Ah, got it. No problem. Let's put in a catheter to relieve the pressure."

She's happy with the plan, tells me she's had catheters many times, including catheterizing herself while at home. She looks at the gown I was sitting next to and asks, "Can I get a new gown, you've been in all those COVID rooms and touched it."

Not a problem. These are stressful times, let's do the easy things if we can. And this is one request that I can fill.

In Room 14 is a young man swollen head to toe, but worst around his eyes and his hands and legs. Robert has had this problem in the past and knows that it's caused by a type of kidney failure. Twenty-five is young for kidney failure. He has curly hair, a red T-shirt decorated with the likeness of President Obama, and blue sweats that have a yellow left knee and red right knee. When I come in the room, Robert has his mask hanging from one ear, and he's on the phone talking. Before I even introduce myself, he asks, "Can you talk to my mom?"

"Sure, put her on speaker."

His mom's raspy smoker's voice fills the room. "How are you, Doctor?"

"I'm good, ma'am, happy to meet you." She explains that he was here yesterday for the same problem but went home because it was his birthday, and he did not want to spend it in the hospital. The three of us discuss a plan to admit him, get him medications to reduce his swelling, and treat the kidney issue that's causing it. She thanks me and tells her son she loves him. I ask if he has any questions.

"Nah, we good."

I notice his right leg is more swollen than his left, something we see with blood clots. I ask, "Is that always more swollen?"

He says, "Yeah, ever since I was shot a couple years ago. Can I get a bed, this chair is uncomfortable, maybe some food?"

I agree, but I warn him that even when we're not too busy it can take a heroic effort to get patients food. It's not a simple request—I have to unravel an administrative snarl.

The gentleman who overdosed is now awake and ready to go home. He needs bus fare. I start a walk around the ED to find Frankie the social worker. The walk is gratifying, and I stop to make eye contact and chat with every colleague I can. After two weeks of social distancing, I've become awkward in conversations. I feel like a puppy begging to be petted. My colleagues who are parents share their struggles with childcare and homeschooling. Others mention their longing for a pint in a bar or a plate of pasta in a restaurant. They wonder when, if ever, they'll feel comfortable doing that again. One lets me know that he won't set foot in a gym for a long time. We're all mourning the loss of our pre-COVID lives, and we all miss each other acutely. I locate Frankie, and she unearths a bus card for the gentleman to get home. On my way back to my desk I find Morris's room empty. His nurse says he didn't wait for the CT, he just rolled out, muttering and angry.

I take a moment to read Monroe's message on my phone. She says she's sorry for the conflict. When she is left hanging, her mind goes to dark places, and I feel the brunt of that. Warmth fills my cheeks and throat. There's more to discuss, but given the distance, FaceTime is all we have. I thank her and let her know I'll call when I get home and leave her with one request: send me funny memes.

From my seat, I see paramedics carrying in a man with blood streaming from his right leg. I jog over to accompany them to his room. His black jeans are wet with blood. Blood has pooled on the paramedics' gurney, and they've cut open his pants to expose his leg. He has wounds on both sides of his calf. I walk with them into Treatment Bay 8, and an internal medicine resident joins us. The paramedics coordinate to move him "on the count of three" from the gurney to a chair as there's no bed available. We help him take off his blood-soaked Air Max shoes and tattered black jeans. He's neither wincing nor angry. He's stoically quiet. "What happened, sir?" I ask.

"I was standing outside a store, shots were fired. I really don't know what happened."

We're the same age—past the age of gunplay—and yet here

he is. He has a normal pulse in the leg, the bones seem stable, and he can move the leg normally. The medicine resident and I decide to do an X-ray, test for a vascular injury, get him pain medication, and send a couple labs. When he goes to a computer to enter the labs, I take another look at the leg. It seems like the bullet went right through the muscle without damaging vessels, nerves, tendons, or ligaments. He was lucky.

The previously dead ER starts to pick up. Another pair of paramedics rush past with a full stretcher. I leave Bay 8 and follow right behind them into Room 12.

"Doc, another OD." I meet a groggy thirty-seven-year-old man in sunglasses, jeans, and a White Sox jersey. The paramedics tell me that he was passed out on a bench before they gave him Narcan.

"Do you know where you are?"

"UIC." By this he means the University of Illinois–Chicago, which is downtown, seven miles north of where we are.

"Nope," I say. "U of C. You're on the South Side."

"Oh, good!" he cries, perking up and clearing his throat. I can see the crust in the corner of his eyes, hear the secretions pooled in his throat. I flinch inwardly and back toward the door as he gurgles.

"Fam, put your mask on. Have you had a COVID test?"

He refuses to answer. "I know I'm negative," he says.

Of course, he doesn't know, and he doesn't want to know for rational reasons that are still wrong. I've seen so many patients who say that same thing: if he's positive, he becomes a pariah and gets shunned. We do for him what we've done for all the other heroin overdoses. We watch them.

Back at my computer area I notice two colleagues chatting.

One is wearing a half-face respirator. It filters 100 percent of three-micron particles and securely covers his face from the nose down. With pink filters on either side and a blue facepiece in the middle, his voice is muffled. He has on protective eye covers, and his grayed and balding pate is visible above. He's relaxed and confident. The other has a blue surgical mask and blue nitrile gloves. His mask hangs below his chin, exposing his face. He's pecking at the keyboard with one gloved hand and eating an apple with the other. One looks ready for pandemic; the other is playing safety charade. I don't judge. We all have lapses. Even if the lapses can be costly.

COVID remains present, even if diminished. The census of patients in the hospital has plateaued and started to decline. Weeks ago, every patient had symptoms, but now only about a third are sick with the virus. We test everyone who will let us and counsel the rest. Our reflexes have become attuned to sneezes and coughs. It feels sometimes like the virus isn't just inside our patients but is restless, clamoring to escape and infect us. We hold it at bay with masks and distance, but after weeks and weeks of this, we're tired and starting to let our guard down. Staff now leave their masks behind for extended periods, sipping drinks at their desks, laughing with arms around each other. Earlier in the pandemic I'd find free food in the ER every day, donated by restaurants or celebrities and labeled "To Our Heroes." That's over, and we are back to scrounging cabinets for Rice Krispies treats. This new phase with fewer COVID cases is a welcome respite. Folks are tired. But we all know it won't last.

My last patient is a very stylish seventy-nine-year-old woman. She's in a silver jacket, silver Nikes, gray jeans, and a gray shirt.

Her curly salt-and-pepper afro frames her face like a halo. She's crying. She came to have a bullet removed. In March a stray bullet flew through her car window, broke her glasses, and lodged above her right eye. She was supposed to go to Ghana the next day and couldn't go—but she didn't miss much because her friends had to return early due to COVID restrictions anyway. Now it's May, and she's tired of having this bullet in her face. I examine her face, but I don't see any scar or swelling. The wound healed, but her head hurts, and she says she can feel the bullet moving in her sinus when she shifts position. It's been scheduled for removal multiple times, but every time the surgery has been canceled by COVID. She can't take it anymore.

"I want it out, and I want it out today."

"The computer says the surgery is scheduled for June," I tell her.

"I can't wait that long. It's driving me crazy!" She's very upset. It's not just the physical suffering but the continued imposition of this shooting on her life. A violent interruption. One moment she was driving, minding her own business, and in the next a bullet changed everything. People come in all the time to have bullets removed. In this case removal wouldn't just stop the pain but close this chapter in her life. I know we can't get it out today. But I can listen. I nod my head as she talks and hold her hand.

Monroe sends a text as I change clothes and prepare to head home. I don't pause to read the *Washington Post* article she sent me about a police shooting; I am too busy rushing to get in the car. Today I feel the usual fatigue and angst from a busy shift but also a quickening inside me at the prospect of this break for freedom at the end of the day. On an almost empty expressway

I'm giddy as I push the speed and turn up the volume. I'm running from the ER. But the ER runs just as fast. It catches me, even on the expressway, and squeezes my mind in its grip. Is there something I missed? Did I forget something? Did I finish everything? The throbbing bass competes with nagging doubts for my attention. I touch the accelerator again and speed off. I'm done. I survived, and so did my patients. Dance music thumps and the streetlights strobe past. I push all memories of the day out of my mind. I'm floating, but I know this feeling won't last. Something is waiting for me in my dreams.

I wake up the next day feeling lost. I'm haunted by memories of the day before, of patients who needed a bite to eat or a speedy bed and I brushed them off. Now I remember the time I couldn't remove a bullet or relieve cancer pain when my patients implored me to. I knew they required more, but I did only what I could. Was it enough? Acquiescing to suffering wounds something deep inside me. I know it, I just don't know what I can do about it.

My growing relationship with Monroe, scrambled by distance and the pandemic, offers no haven. I have grappled with relationships before, sometimes killing them as they become challenging rather than struggling through; other times they've been waylaid by a move or an illness. They say, "There are plenty of fish in the sea," but once I catch mine, I still have to hold on to her. While physical distancing and work push Monroe and me apart, I feel myself hardening to her, just as I have to my patients whose needs I cannot meet. I sit up in bed and contemplate the day. I think about calling her after I have a cup of coffee.

The whir of beans grinding and the whistle of the boiling

water pot signal the beginning of a new day. With the first couple sips of coffee, last night's failures and the growing distance
between me and Monroe sink in. I will try my hardest to care
for patients and to love Monroe, and in both cases it may not be
enough. I gather myself to remain intentional and vulnerable.
The only way to have love and to hold on to hope is to run
toward her even when we're falling apart. Just as the only way
to care for sick people teetering on the edge of life and death
is to give them everything I have, even as they slip away. In both
cases that exposure may leave me full of hurt, but there isn't any
other way—the pain is the only path to the grace and transcendence that come from a true human connection. To be open to
that touch—human to human—means remaining open to loss.
Over and over again. I want to weep for all the losses over so
many years. But crying now wouldn't do any good.

I dial Monroe.

7

Dear Robert,

You came to me swollen because of your kidney problem. It was the day after your birthday, and I talked with you and your mom about what we could do to treat your puffiness. Twenty-five is so young to have these health issues. In the years when most people brim with strength and endurance, you are forced to navigate your world with diminished stamina. Your birthday celebration was forced to compete with a hospitalization. You've been robbed of so much well-being at such a young age, first by the kidney disorder and then by the complications of being shot. Unfortunately, you are not alone—serious and chronic illnesses strike young people more often in our community than in most. I can't fix that. As you might remember, I couldn't even get you a warm meal when you wanted it. But at least I can help you understand your health and why young people like you on the South Side have so many good, healthy years stolen away from them.

On your good days, I'm sure you can feel the wonder of the human body—the wonder of *your specific* body. Interrelated organs, balanced intake and waste, locomotion, and sensors that allow us to see, feel, and hear. We are miracles. When we're born, we are weak and defenseless, entirely dependent. After being nurtured through a risky first year, we grow through childhood, dodging injuries and infection until we reach the peak of our physical potential in early adulthood.

When we were together, I wanted to talk about more than just your kidney disease. I had the impression that you believed the ailment was unfair but inevitable. But to understand your predicament, we'll need to take a step back. I don't know if this will help, but I think you should understand the source of your pain.

Our bodies are our most important endowment. Across our life span, we dream and hope, live and love, build and grow as much as our strength allows. As we age and accumulate wear, our bodies falter and recover, our strength and comfort fluctuating year over year. At some point illness and injury inevitably catch up to all of us, our decline becomes irreversible, and we die. Disease, infections, accidents, violence, and the natural decline of age end each of our lives in our own time. But the trajectory of our health doesn't always move in the same direction. We experience health misfortunes—but the way we care for our priceless bodies after a setback can tip the equilibrium back toward health.

Your body, like many bodies on the South Side, began accumulating injury and illness before the bodies of your peers on the North Side, and unlike your peers, you had fewer chances to recover and return to your prior health.

Health. We use the word all the time, but what is it, really? The World Health Organization provides an aspirational definition of health: "a state of complete physical, mental and social well-being and not merely the absence of disease or infirmity." By this definition, none of us is ever fully healthy. Whether we witness violence as a child or we're stressed as an adult, consume too little food while young or too much when we're grown, compounding and interacting physical and social exposures beginning in gestation and progressing over time shape our bodies into a state just short of complete well-being. When these functions work well enough, we call ourselves healthy and are free to pursue meaning in our lives.

You are twenty-five. These should be the healthiest years of your life. Your kidney problem is a chronic disorder that came too soon and struck too hard. Worse, you were shot, leaving you with a swollen and painful leg. Nobody should be violently attacked. I can't imagine what that feels like. Even with your chronic conditions, you retain consider-able reserve, and I'm so happy you seized the chance to celebrate a landmark birthday. You know you aren't alone. You must have noticed all the dialysis centers on the South Side. Considering how common kidney disease is around here, I wouldn't be surprised if you aren't even the only person in your family with kidney problems. I also sus-pect you know others who have been shot. I bet you wonder if you were destined to be sick because it just runs in your family, and maybe you think being shot was just bad luck. Maybe you're right, and these problems were unavoidable. But not for the reasons you might think.

In every measure of health status, Black people like you, here on the South Side, lag when compared to white people like those on the North Side. Over a lifetime, biological, behavioral, and social experi-ences hasten or delay the erosion of our bodies. We grow our under-standing of these processes every year and have made significant progress to address many common ailments—sharply curbing infant mortality, curing many infections, and improving the quality and length of millions of lives. In this same course, obesity has become so common in America that it is the norm rather than the exception. Despite our knowledge, we cannot evenly distribute progress—health disorders more often affect Black than white folks, more often affect poor than rich folks. You and your family members with kidney disorders—should they exist—are not simply unlucky. And you weren't shot purely because you were in the wrong place at the wrong time. There are patterns to these illnesses and injuries. The factors that lead to worse health on the South Side than on the North Side can be seen more easily when we consider a prominent and well-studied chronic condition: diabetes.

Diabetes is a disorder in which blood sugar becomes too elevated and the body is unable to use it as fuel.

We process glucose with the help of insulin, and diabetes is a malady where the body is unable to regulate insulin. It comes in two distinct flavors. In type 1 diabetes, which is more associated with the developing years of life, the body stops producing insulin. In type 2 diabetes, which is far more linked to adult behaviors, the body becomes unable to use the insulin that is around. Insulin tells our cells to grab the sugar that's floating in our bloodstream, allowing our cells to use it for fuel and lowering our blood sugar levels. Insulin's role in diabetes was discovered in 1921. This breakthrough in how cells and hormones work together to shape health and disease would earn Frederick Banting and John Macleod the Nobel Prize for Physiology or Medicine two years later. These molecular insights reveal what is going on inside an individual's body but fail to predict which groups are likely to fall ill or why. Understanding insulin doesn't tell me why Black people disproportionately suffer from diabetes. Why is it more likely for people with low incomes to have diabetes? Why does diabetes cluster in certain neighborhoods? The answers to these questions will help us to understand the complicated interactions between our bodies and the society we live in.

You live on the South Side of Chicago, the same community I grew up in. The natural and built environments of the South Side—everything from the infrastructure of the city streets to the quality of the water we drink—determine our vitality, just as they do in any neighborhood. In fact, 5 to 10 percent of your overall health is determined by the environment. Elevated levels of pollution from nearby factories increase the burden of asthma in a given area, while physical barriers such as buildings without ramp access or elevators take their toll on people with disabilities. The presence of lead in the water and community violence influence the health status of young people. These conditions are neither evenly nor randomly distributed. For example, the presence or absence of healthful food options determines the prevalence of obesity and diabetes. In 2010 almost 10 percent of Americans lived in food deserts—areas with limited access to affordable food that is nutritious. These zones were almost exclusively low-income communities without the spending power to attract supermarkets. That same poverty limited the ability of residents to travel to other neighborhoods for healthy food. In Chicago, Black people make up approximately 30 percent of the population—but almost 80 percent of the people who live in food deserts, and most of those people are right here on the South Side. While diabetes is a disorder of blood sugar, the link between poverty, race, and diabetes is environmental. Remember how much of your overall health is derived from the environment—as much as 10 percent. Unless you are able to move to a healthier area, these outcomes are entirely circumstantial and out of your control.

Many people who have problems like yours believe they will solve them by changing their diet and exercising more. And they are partially right—our behaviors do affect our health. Smoking habits, sleep and exercise patterns, safer sexual practices are the kinds of actions that contribute 30 to 40 percent to our physical and mental well-being. But even then, outside factors weigh on us. While your use of seat belts and condoms, your consumption of vegetables and cocaine, seem to be solely under your control, they're also compelled by your circumstances.

For instance, many chronic conditions like diabetes are shaped by behaviors like smoking and exercise. Smoking, in turn, is driven by what's advertised and available to you in stores. You might be surprised to learn that menthol cigarettes, for instance, have been forced on you and your neighborhood through predatory marketing over a period of several decades. Regular exercise requires leisure time that is in short supply for working folks who don't have a lot of control over their schedules or who have to cobble together two or more jobs to make ends meet. In Avalon Park, an hour's walk south of the hospital, 34 percent of adults do not get regular exercise, compared to 12 percent in the North Side's Lincoln Park—but 30 percent smoke, compared to 9 percent, respectively. Healthful options are plentiful up on the North Side and scarce around here. People in your community can select only between risky and riskier choices.

Even further from your control are your social circumstances. Context like your family's wealth and educational attainment contributes 20 to 30 percent to your health status. Our early childhood development, education, exposure to discrimination, and culture all impact development and personal health. Concentrated poverty, low education, and the inability to accrue and then transfer wealth result in poor health and lower quality of life. On the other hand, wealth, high social status, and good education protect from illness and injury. In Chicago we see huge gulfs in these circumstances from one community to another. In the South Side's Englewood neighborhood, 25 percent are unemployed, compared to 3 percent in the North Side's Lakeview. And in Englewood 23 percent do not graduate from high school, while only 2 percent miss this educational landmark in Lakeview. A map of Chicago's residential segregation is also a map of its educational attainment, wealth, diabetes—and COVID cases.

Families on the South Side have less education, income, and wealth, which contributes to diminished access to goods, services, and legal protections. Opportunities and safeguards are concentrated on the North Side. As a result, Black people, who densely populate the South Side, are forced to endure a gauntlet of health risks: jobs that maim, food that sickens, air that chokes, and guns that kill. This would be a simple story of winners and losers, except there is no competition—not a fair one, at least. The contest was decided at birth, and this tournament trades in the most important of human endowments—our health. In Chicago that means folks who come to me in the ED from the nearby Grand Boulevard neighborhood are eight times as likely to have a limb amputated for diabetes as those who live in the Loop. Men who live next door, in violent Englewood, have a life expectancy of fifty-nine years, compared to ninety in Streeterville, and people in Englewood are nine times more likely to be hospitalized for diabetes than those in River North.

Robert, you were shot in your neighborhood and came down with a serious kidney disease, all before you turned twenty-five. While I know you feel like you should have been home the day you were shot, or maybe eaten differently to avoid the kidney disease, in fact you probably had very little control over these awful turns in your health. The reasons that your kidneys were more likely to fail and that you were more likely to get shot involve complicated interplays between you and the society you live in. A combination of behaviors that are shaped by your neighborhood, the environment that you live in, and society itself put you and your entire community at risk. Fewer guns, more jobs, better food options, reduced environmental toxins, and a host of other improvements could have allowed you to celebrate your twenty-fifth in style rather than waiting for a hospital visit. Nobody chooses to have their lives shortened, but individuals have a hard time changing the segregation in their neighborhood, the social status they were born into, or their relationship with discrimination.

Many people look at the poor health in their family and community and think it's inherited. You might think that your genes are responsible for your kidney problem. In fact, many people in medicine also believe these patterns in Black people must result from something encoded deep inside that is passed from parents to children. I want you to know, this might be partially true, but it's not entirely true. Yes, your physical structure and bodily functions—from bone density to coordination to height—have components that are encoded in your genome. We learned about genetics in grade school with the inheritance patterns of pea plant flowers. We did those two-by-two tables to help it sink in and looked around to apply these insights to eye color and height in humans. This makes good sense, but when we apply the same logic to human disease it quickly falls apart—your genetic makeup determines about only 20 percent of your health.

Some ailments like Huntington's disease, Down syndrome, cystic fibrosis, and sickle cell anemia are wholly inherited—if a person has been given these genes by their parents, their fate is clear. Beyond that handful of disorders, our genes are expressed in concert with our environment. While we may have the capacity to be tall, our childhood diet has a say in our adult height. Your propensity for diabetes or kidney disease is not a direct inheritance like Huntington's disease. Rather, it is a risk determined in association with other external factors, like a lifetime of diet and exercise along with a thousand other exposures and protections. Even your life span is only 10 percent a question of inheritance. The other 90 percent is determined by society, culture, and experiences. Did you know that male-female partners who are related by a social bond like marriage—and thus have a similar lifestyle, but very different genes—have better correlated life spans than male-female siblings who share genetics? Shared exposure to wealth/poverty trumps DNA.

We've long sought the genes that encode "race" for their power to mediate health and illness. These pursuits, carried across centuries now, have always come up empty. While there is genetic inheritance that reflects our ancestry, race as a category is arbitrarily defined and changes in time and across space. In 1930 the U.S. Census counted Mexicans, but ten years later Mexicans were folded into the "white" category. Would a 1930s Mexican have their risk of diabetes redefined along with their racial category? By looking to link genetic or molecular components to this haphazard grouping we call race, too often we ignore the larger inherited health factors that are both in plain view and under our societal control.

Societal status and practices are also transferred across generations. I've already described how neighborhoods shape our health with food "deserts," but they also predict whether children can walk to good schools and whether gun violence is prevalent. These conditions are also inherited, as most adults—especially those with less education or lower incomes—do not venture far from their communities. I live only seven miles from where I grew up, and I bet you are even closer. Black people in general are more likely to live close to their parents than white people. It is often inherited wealth—not income—that protects Americans from working and living in dangerous conditions, conditions that become even more risky when pandemics arrive. Without inherited wealth it is much more difficult to leave a dangerous situation for a safer one. In 1863, Black Americans owned 0.5 percent of the national wealth, and in 2019 they possessed just over 1.5 percent, growing in roughly the same percentage as the growth of our overall population. Over the years, I've been helped considerably by my parents. I met your mom. She was deeply engaged in your care, and I bet she helps you too. But I haven't benefited from a financial inheritance, and I bet you haven't either. These inherited, nonbiological variables, like wealth, a home, the connections to start a business, and protection from legal consequences, help explain why the South Side is sicker than the North Side, as well as the practices that reproduce this pattern across the generations.

The fact that there is no biological underpinning for race helps debunk proposed natural mechanisms for health inequities. Still, too many physicians and scientists accept that the inequities around us emerge from inside the bodies we treat, rather than in relation to prevailing societal structures or systems. This leads to the belief that those inequities can be solved with piecemeal interventions. And don't get me wrong: piecemeal interventions—whether by physicians or researchers or each of us as individuals—have real value. But they are insufficient. We've put the onus on individuals for their healthy behaviors, their environmental influences, and their social circumstances, and in doing so we've absolved society. We all need to do our best for ourselves and—as physicians—for our individual, one-at-a-time patients. But it is society that shapes the population-wide patterns that we see. Our public policies and public health decisions shape our city, the distribution of resources inside it, the environments we live in, the choices available to us, and, ultimately, our health.

These societal decisions create the inequities we see when we compare the North Side to the South Side.

We have set up a system where we've stratified our city by race
and taken our best collective health assets and transferred them to
the North Side. Over centuries, Chicago's segregation has distributed
materials and resources, opportunities and restrictions. The neighborhoods we live in define our social networks, the foods we eat, our
wealth and education, our employment and housing. Transmitted
across generations, this hierarchy dictates which people have the
best opportunities for health and for illness. It is our society, having
sorted materials, that ensures white people on the North Side enjoy
long, disease-free lives, while Black people on the South Side face
shorter lives full of disability. The abbreviated, more painful lives of
Black folks and the longer, more robust lives white folks experience
do not simply exist side by side: they are linked.

You were unlucky not only on the day you were shot but also on
the day you were born. Your kidneys failed, and you were shot in large
part because of the neighborhood, city, and country you live in, not
because of things you did—or even had the power to do. Today I got
to help you end your day just a little healthier than when you started.
You are young, but your illnesses mean you will have a lower quality
of life and shorter life span than your peers. I know it must be frustrating to think that so little of your health is in your control, but that's not
why I'm telling you this. I want you to know that your illness is not your
fault—and all of those other people you know, sick or shot or dying
slowly, are also fighting a harder battle than they know against op-
ponents they'll never see. But it's not unwinnable. I hope you find it
liberating to know that a healthier future for the South Side is possible
with a more just and equal society—the policies that misallocate resources and reinforce the boundaries of segregation can be changed.

Beating ourselves up only distracts us from the fight we need to have. Until then, I hope this letter has provided you with a little information to help you understand why our communities are so sick and how to make your voice heard.

Onward,

tlf

8

JULY 4, 2020

IT'S BEEN A WEEK since I've been in the Emergency Department. In the interim Chicago has warmed up. It's now a balmy 89 with high humidity. But the heat in Chicago is always a mixed blessing, and this holiday weekend, violence spiked in proportion to the temperature. I check the police scanner on my way in to my 10 A.M. shift to anticipate what will confront me in the ED. Yesterday, July 3, while I strolled outdoors with my sister and played with my niece, eleven people were shot and one killed. The cadence of violence escalated in the wee hours—by morning another ten were shot, three killed. As much of the North Side enjoyed a socially distant holiday, the tantrums of gunfire on the South and West Sides were evident to them only on the scrolling chyrons. In all, twenty-five people were shot in the first twenty-four hours of the holiday weekend.

On my way through the back hallways to the scrub machine I bump into one of the attending trauma surgeons. A clean-cut ex-military surgeon, he is out of his scrubs and in athletic shorts emblazoned with the yellow Marines logo. He's masked, and his wire glasses frame bleary eyes. I greet him with a quick "What's up, Dirk?" With his brown bald head reflecting the fluorescent light overhead, he shrugs and says, "I'm a zombie. Last night was busy, one shooting after the next. It rolled right into this morning. One dead already." Usually his body language reflects military discipline, but today his shoulders aren't at attention. Socially distanced about ten feet away, I shake my head.

"When are you back?"

"I'm on backup call today."

"I hope you get some rest and a meal before you have to come back." As he heads out, my legs feel suddenly heavy, the floor transformed into sand.

I head over to the vending machine to gather scrubs, and an unfamiliar doctor follows me to the alcove. There aren't many Black doctors, so I greet her but don't spend time chatting. It looks like the new interns have arrived.

With fresh scrubs on, I head to the ED. My protection is complete, with a blue surgical mask and a purple cloth head covering made for me by my colleague Phillis. I am the double coverage doctor today, extra hands responsible for trauma airways and psychiatric patients. I'm not replacing anyone, so there's nobody tired and waiting for my arrival in order to leave, just a colleague who needs help covering the rooms. I check the computer and find the track board sparsely populated, nobody in the waiting room, and many open treatment areas. Despite a bloody night, today starts with calm.

After I perform my ritual area cleaning, I explore the ED. I review Rooms 24 to 30; most are empty, and the staff are chat-

ting or surfing the internet. The mood is low-key, and the psychiatric rooms are uncharacteristically vacant. My survey
continues to the trauma bay, where I bump into the new resident doctor I saw at the scrub machine.

"Hey, I'm Thomas Fisher, one of the ED attendings," I say,
offering her an elbow bump. She's my height, in a mask and
goggles, and her long braids are hidden under a disposable bouf-
fant hair cover.

"I'm Renee. This is my first day." I noticed from her ID that
she's an emergency medicine resident.

"Oh, you're one of ours?" For decades we've stood out from
our peer training programs with our commitment to training
Black doctors. There were years when that lineage was in jeop-
ardy, so meeting the next generation of the tradition is stirring.

"I am. I'm rotating on trauma surgery this month."

"Welcome. I'm so happy you're here. We won't work together
much until next year. And then we'll be thick as thieves. Until then,
let me know if you need anything." She thanks me and I walk out
of the trauma bay, ready to see patients and feeling optimistic.

I learn later that Renee is from Connecticut and was trained
on the East Coast. This is her first time living outside of the
Northeast. In Chicago, Black folks are mostly descendants of
migrants from the Deep South, as opposed to the East Coast,
where Black people from the coastal South are mixed in with
other Black immigrants from across the diaspora. She's going to
care for a population that will be familiar but different than the
Black communities she is accustomed to. Her patients will tell
her they're proud of her. They'll offer to introduce her to their
grandsons and share secrets reserved for family. She has a very
special three years ahead of her.

My shift overlaps with a peer of fifteen years' duration. Janet is the residency director, and today, along with her blue scrubs, she wears black socks with red and white polka dots and a matching red, white, and black surgical cap over her blond hair. She's a social savant with perfect recall of everyone's name and story after meeting them the first time. When we work together shifts flow quickly, with easy conversation. We're more than ten feet apart, at computers adjacent to one another, our desks separated by a walkway. As with all ED conversations, we start with the virus—which has turned her process of interviewing, screening, and onboarding residents virtual. Then we move on to the second most common topic these days: leadership.

Last night, she told me, she watched President Trump give a speech at Mount Rushmore surrounded by his usual fanfare and arrests of indigenous protestors, military flyovers, flag-waving. It was a very American event in some of the most worrisome ways. One of the members of the presidential entourage tested positive and had to drive back to D.C.

"How is it that the president has never tested positive?" she asks.

It's a question that has annoyed me, too. "I have no idea," I say. "It's remarkable. He's surrounded by folks who have COVID, and he doesn't wear masks but has still avoided the infection."

"Given what happened to Boris Johnson," Janet says, "if he got sick maybe America would actually take this thing seriously. What's happening right now is some bullshit." In late March the British prime minister announced that he had contracted COVID-19, deepening the British response. We agree that Trump is probably the beneficiary of high-volume testing, tracking,

and social distancing. If only the rest of the country—with
2.8 million cases and more than 122,000 dead at this moment—
had the same luxury.

Life has changed for everyone. We haven't seen each other
socially in months. We've started to perceive normal behaviors
and familiar places as threats. Hugging, dining out, and socializing in bars no longer feel safe. But in the ED, things feel different for us—different even from how things felt back in March
and May. Some of the doctors and staff get right up close with
COVID-positive patients in haphazard equipment, and it seems
quite normal, just a neighbor with a fever and cough. Not me. I
am fastidious with PPE in the ED. When others let their masks
slip, my anxiety rises. I remain at my desk a comfortable distance away from Janet, even if it means anyone can eavesdrop
on our conversation. The COVID paradox has undermined my
instincts. I feel insane when I avoid normal mingling but hold
my guard in common situations where others are relaxed.

An hour into my shift, I have my first patient. In Room 29
awaits Ms. Crawford, a seventy-one-year-old woman. Bryan, her
resident, tells me that she can't breathe when she lies down or
walks even short distances. She was recently admitted for the
same problem, and on discharge her medications were changed
from three diuretic pills a day to one. After being home for a
week she noticed her legs becoming tight and swollen, and then
her breathing issues returned.

I find her with her salt-and-pepper hair styled into curls and
her church-lady glasses on a chain around her neck.

"Good morning, ma'am. I'm Dr. Fisher. How are you feeling?"

"I'm okay, baby." Her accent is Southern and warm. Ms.

Crawford is well groomed and neatly dressed in a patterned dress under her gown. Reminds me of my grandmother, who always presented herself meticulously put together in public to ensure the best possible service.

"I'm doing what I'm told," she tells me. "I'm trying to get better, but it doesn't seem like I've been able to." As she takes me through her winding path, I sense weariness. She shares with me that besides the leg swelling and trouble breathing she's had back pain for quite some time, and two weeks ago she got an injection to help.

"Do I have to stay?" Her voice shows hesitancy.

"I think you might want to. I won't make you do anything, but it might be easier to stay. I just want to be sure you're comfortable and that we figure out what's going on with your breathing."

"Okay, baby. You just do whatever. I'd rather get it all done now. I do not want to have to come back *again*. Help me feel better." I've heard that familiar "baby" from elders my entire life. She is not kin to me, but she's as familiar as summers in Kansas and Thanksgivings in Detroit. If she is like my grandma, she's had doctors dismiss her complaints, doing only what's expedient rather than what's necessary. If nothing else, I will honor her trust in me, I will help her feel safe, I will make her feel better. And I will make sure she knows how to stay out of the hospital. If her breathing problem is as simple as needing more medications, we'll fix it, and if not, we'll figure out what the problem is. Patients like this are the reason I'm a doctor— and the reason I'm a doctor in this specific ED.

"I will, I promise." I pat her hand and step out to my workstation to update Bryan.

Bryan is a rising second-year resident and one of the stronger doctors in his class. He's capably transitioning from his internship year, during which interns are expected to need help, to his second year, when residents are expected to provide help. Everybody knows the interns have everything to learn, and the riskiest new doctors are those who think that they know everything, but Bryan knew enough to ask for help. So does our new intern this shift, whose name is Dania. She's from Massachusetts and is competently and nervously sorting one patient after the next. My challenge is gauging how much assistance the second-year residents need without stepping on their toes.

In through the ambulance bay arrive two paramedics with an older woman on their stretcher. She is quietly but visibly grimacing. They're headed to Room 34, and I hop out of my chair to meet them there.

"Hey, folks. What's going on?"

Contextual information direct from the on-scene paramedics is invaluable. I'm expecting a report so that we can get to work. The paramedics ignore me, so I try again: "Hey, there. Is she sick?" The two paramedics and three nurses are all in masks and focused on sliding this older woman from the gurney to the ED bed. Wrapped in blankets head to toe, she's in a patterned blue house coat, and a blue surgical mask covers her nose and mouth. Her graying hair is covered by a light blue turban. It takes a third inquiry before they respond.

"Yeah, Doc. My bad. She fell outside, and the neighbors called 911 because of her leg."

"What's wrong with her leg?"

"I don't know. She fell and hurt it."

"Did she hit her head?"

"I don't know."

It's like pulling teeth out of these paramedics to get an idea of what's going on. While most paramedics are great, some don't care; others don't know. I think these two are not used to a doctor being curious about the circumstances of the people they transport, but I always ask—they often give me helpful context before I begin my examination. It's frustrating to have to push them to get more, and it makes me wonder, with some concern, how much they're paying attention. But it is what it is. With one more direct prompt they divulge that she's eighty-four and that she stumbled and twisted and hurt her leg. After the spill, she was unable to get up. A neighbor who saw her fall called 911. Her leg looks normal down to about the knee, and then below the right knee her foot is turned at 90 degrees to the left. I quickly discover that she's hard of hearing. Before COVID I'd get close to someone like this, talk right into her ear or give her my stethoscope and speak quietly into the bell. But now I have to shout yes or no questions to get information. I order X-rays and a CT of her head and neck since I don't know if she fully understands my questions. I don't want to miss any brain injuries in case it turns out that she did hit her head. I shout to her that her leg looks like it might need surgery. The nurse and Bryan and I debate the best pain medications. Fentanyl works well but can make an older woman confused and constipated; ketorolac isn't good on her kidneys; Tylenol is very safe but may not give her much relief. No perfect answers here, so we decide on Tylenol and an injection of lidocaine right into the fracture.

I leave the room, wash my hands, and walk directly across the

department over to Room 25. The patient in Room 25 is an older
gentleman with a scruffy black-and-white beard and a "Chevy"
trucker hat perched on his white afro. His name is Jones.

"Hey, watch out, be careful there. I missed the urinal."

I look where he's pointing and see a puddle of urine on the
floor.

"Thanks for warning me. By the way, can you pull your mask
up over your nose and mouth?"

I feel like the mask hall monitor, but he pulls his mask over
his face without objection. Mr. Jones complains that his right
hand is painful and swollen and that he can't hold things anymore.

"It hurts all the way up to my shoulder, Doc. Oooh. Damn."

He grimaces as he tries to move the shoulder. The pain started
a couple days ago with no clear provocation. Although he has
plenty of medical problems, it's not clear if one of them caused
this. "Take a look, Doc," he says, showing me a right hand with
fingers fat like sausages. He can move it, and it's got a normal
pulse, but its cartoonish size has made him clumsy. It's no wonder he missed the urinal.

I look for his intern, Dania, to see what she thinks is going on.
She's appropriately worried about a blood clot somewhere in
his shoulder or neck. We decide to get labs and an ultrasound to
search for the blockage, but it's a holiday and the ultrasound is
unavailable. Instead, we'll give him a blood thinner and have
him come back as soon as it's available. It is not optimal to send
him home with risky medications and no clear diagnosis. If he
falls and bumps his head, a blood thinner changes a minor inconvenience into devastating bleeding. But without the test it's
the best we can do. Dania is worried about the possibilities.

She's got the anxiety of being new and wanting to do well while sorting out a challenge full of uncertainty and inadequate solutions. We set up a sequence of blood tests that would find other potential triggers for his swelling and then schedule a clear follow-up plan to get the ultrasound done. Together we go back to talk with Mr. Jones.

I've been in the Emergency Department about three and a half hours now, and the blasting air conditioning has me yearning for sun. I walk through the nearly empty waiting room and nod to the chatting security team on my way outside. Usually there are Chicago Police cars parked on the block and family members and patients leaning against the building talking and smoking while they wait. Today is hazy and warm, and the block has a single campus police car and no smokers. The quiet reminds me of that same street seven nights earlier, when I cared for a psychotic man surrounded by police.

That night a nurse alerted me that the police needed me outside to help deescalate a situation with a patient. On my way outside the nurse quickly introduced me to the patient's dad, who told me that his son, Art, was off his bipolar medications. He said that Art had stopped sleeping at night and this evening had taken a rideshare up to the northern suburbs, where he tried to break into Scottie Pippen's old house. When a home alarm went off, Art called his father for a ride. He drove an hour and found him hiding in the bushes. He'd been helping Art deal with his illness for years and brought him directly here, but Art was now refusing to come inside. Given his erratic behavior, his dad engaged the hospital security and campus police to keep him from absconding or doing something dangerous.

It was 4 A.M. On the sidewalk across the street from the ED

entrance streetlights illuminated a man in a white T-shirt and shorts with his back against the fence. The first light of the rising sun was changing the midnight sky to indigo, and nesting birds were signaling a new day with their scattered calls. Eight police officers in various poses of readiness surrounded him; their heads turned to look toward me as I joined the circle. The captain spoke up: "He's refusing to come in, Doc. What do you want us to do?"

Just a couple of weeks after George Floyd was tortured to death on video, I found myself accidentally in command of a phalanx of cops surrounding a mentally ill man. I didn't answer the captain but kept my eyes on the fellow at the center of this crescent.

"Hey, bruh. I'm Dr. Fisher. I spoke to your dad, he told me what's going on. He's worried about you."

"HE LYING!"

"Ah, word? Really? Let's sort that out. Come on inside, and we can discuss this together."

"Go in where? Nah, I'm good. I'll just go on home."

His speech was pressured and loud.

"Art, it's chilly out here, and you're in shorts. Let's take a breath. We don't have to do this here."

"I see these cops. They're going to kill me! That's all they do! But I'm rich. I'm supposed to be able to go! Don't let them do this."

We were in a standoff, and after ten minutes outside wearing only scrubs I was shivering, either from the chill or maybe adrenaline. This man was psychotic and couldn't be reasoned with. I looked to the sky, considering what else I could do. Steam wafted lazily from the smokestack of a building behind him, and the sun just wouldn't come up any faster.

The captain stepped in. "Hey, Art. We had a good conversation. The doctor needs to talk to you. Let's go inside."

Art refused.

I said, "Art, I'm going to ask the officers to help you come on in. Look, we're creating a commotion." And I pointed to a TV camera crew setting up at the end of the block. Four police moved in, showed him their gloved hands, and then gently put them on his arms and shoulders. As though they'd broken a spell, Art quietly stopped resisting and came along without pulling, arguing, or dragging. We repeated this process of a warning from me, then police hands gently on his arms at every transition point along the way, from the hospital hallway into a room, then out of his clothes and into a gown, and finally into accepting a shot of antipsychotic medicine. With each confrontation, he triggered me with an insulting word, tone, or posture, but I kept the conversation going as best I could. He needed me to respond, to feel heard, to feel respected and considered. Over forty-five minutes of talking, deescalating, touching him, and refusing to take his bait, we got him in, medicated and calm.

Today, I stand in the doorway for fifteen minutes enjoying the sun and thinking back on that night. I'm warm and not a single patient heads past me for care. Now that COVID has scared off a lot of patients, there are more pauses from the usual frenetic pace in which to reflect. COVID has given me something I've never had before in the ER: time.

I return inside just as the trauma alarm goes off: "Code Yellow, Level Two, seven minutes away." With that, I understand an ambulance is on the way with a trauma patient who has a serious but not life-threatening injury, and I have seven minutes to prepare. I change my regular mask for an N95, then don a face shield, gloves, and impermeable gown. I meet Bryan at the head of the bed in the trauma bay. We prepare by discussing the things that we need for an emergency airway. Airway issues are the most immediate life threat. Until we know for sure that the patient is stable, we need to be fully prepared to act immediately. He turns on the suction to clear blood and vomit, gathers special tools to open the airway of an unconscious person, and assembles intubation supplies. When we need these tools, we can't stop to search for them, they must be on hand immediately. If we had heard "Code Yellow, Level One," we would know that the injury is life-threatening, and our preparation would extend to drawing up medications into syringes and opening additional tools to open a chest or insert a large-bore IV.

Paramedics roll in a twenty-three-year-old woman on a spine board, wearing a cervical collar. She's in denim shorts and a tank top and is screaming wildly, "My leg my leg my leg MY LEG my leg." One of the paramedics was a tech in the ED for many years; he gives me an elbow bump and reports: "S'up Fish, this is Yesinia. She was in a high-speed crash into a wall on the expressway. Stable vital signs, deformed right leg." He shows pictures of the car on his phone. The front end is crushed like an accordion; the driver's door hangs open, revealing a limp airbag inside. The windshield is spiderwebbed, and the steering wheel is bent. Yesinia is frenzied from pain or maybe intoxicated and unable to communicate with us. The techs quickly cut her clothes free, start an IV, and connect her to the monitor. While I stand at the head of the bed with Bryan, the trauma intern,

Charisse, examines the patient's bare body, listens for even breaths, checks for symmetric pulses, looks for signs of bleeding, and assesses her capacity to follow commands, sharing her findings aloud as she proceeds. Besides a buckled right leg, the patient doesn't appear to have any other injuries. But that right leg is a problem: the bones are protruding through the skin near the ankle, and her foot is twisted at an absurd angle. We give her 50 micrograms of fentanyl for pain and one milligram of lorazepam to calm her down and then she's off to the CT scan.

Before I can leave the trauma bay the next one is on the way. Code Yellow, Level Two, five minutes. In comes the same paramedic who was vague about his report earlier. He unloads a gray-haired, disheveled older man. With eyes closed, the gentleman is lying quietly on a spine board, wearing a neck immobilization collar. Peacefully asleep or bleeding into his brain? Next to me is the attending trauma surgeon. She is erect in posture, arms crossed, hair in a ponytail. She barks out impatiently, "What do you have for us?" The paramedic doesn't respond. "What are the vital signs?!" The paramedic is once again mysteriously uncommunicative. Finally, maybe after he has gathered his thoughts, he turns to us to offer a report: eighty-nine-year-old man found at the bottom of stairs, unresponsive. Nobody witnessed him fall, but neighbors saw him at the bottom of a flight of stairs, not moving, and assumed that he was injured. The patient is groggy but wakes up when pinched. His breath smells so strongly of alcohol I can recognize it through my N95. We can't find any obvious injuries, and his vital signs are stable. He falls back to sleep, and it takes another pinch to wake him again to ask more questions. Maybe he's just drunk, but drunk people often fall downstairs and badly hurt themselves. He's stable enough and heads to the CT scanner right behind the woman with the broken ankle.

This is a mysterious shift. Shootings clogged the evening news and exhausted the trauma surgeons, but there's no sign of that now. Here in the hottest and most violent weekend in years, thankfully we haven't seen a single one. It's as though it's not happening. It's time to catch up.

Bryan lets me know that the woman with the swollen legs who is having trouble breathing has been admitted and that the hard-of-hearing woman with the broken ankle is headed for surgery.

Dania comes to me anxious about proceeding with her patient with the swollen arm. Dania and I discuss her discomfort with acting on incomplete information. It's normal to be unsure. Sometimes you'll act wrongly, and that's part of what we do. It's also one of the things that robs me of sleep when I go home. Her diligence suggests she will have the same experience.

After her CT scans, Yesinia, the woman from the car accident, is moved to Room 36. She's still screaming in pain from her right leg and, probably, from the terror of running her car into a wall. It turns out her ankle requires emergency surgery, but first we have to try to pull the bones back into alignment. Moving fractured bones is extremely painful, and the decisive movements required to rearrange her ankle will be torture without sedation. I'm going to give her a combination of ketamine and propofol for the procedure, two powerful medications that have some resonance from the news. Ketamine was the dissociative medication that killed Elijah McClain. McClain was wearing a ski mask and flailing his arms to music when a neighbor called the police about a man who looked "sketchy." He resisted when confronted and at the direction of Aurora, Colorado, police, paramedics overdosed him with 500 milligrams. He suffocated and died.

An overdose of propofol is what killed Michael Jackson. His personal doctor stopped his breathing with an injection intended to be a sleep aid. I will use a fraction of the massive doses given to McClain and Jackson to safely protect Yesinia from a terribly painful experience.

We set up our materials and go through a checklist to ensure it's the right patient, the right doses, and the right procedure. Oxygen goes on her face, and we connect a sensor to measure her exhaled carbon dioxide. The nurse pushes the ketamine, and then I dose her with propofol. Yesinia goes into a twilight of sleep. Unfortunately, despite pulling and pushing the broken ankle, the senior orthopedics resident can't realign the bones. As Yesinia groans and squeals, he twists and jerks them into the correct position, but they just keep slipping out again. This means the fracture is worse than the X-ray shows. The longer it's out of place, the more likely that the broken bone will not get enough blood flow. Sweaty from the effort, the resident calls to prepare the operating room. The patient's best shot is an operation as soon as possible. When Yesinia wakes up fully from sedation, she doesn't remember having her ankle bent. I let her know the orthopedics team will soon come talk to her about surgery, and I walk to my desk to write notes.

Working on holidays is frustrating. I'd rather be partying with friends and family, but the ER is 24/7/365—someone has to be there. Over the years I've done my fair share. The only redemption is the food on holiday shifts. As an intern I worked a twenty-four-hour trauma shift on Thanksgiving. That November there was a heroin war on the West Side of Chicago. So many people were shot that I'd had to change my blood-saturated scrubs multiple times a shift. Without two consecutive days off that entire month, there was never time to rest, to run errands and socialize, and when something had to give, it was always the socializing. As a result, almost all my human interaction happened at work. That Thanksgiving everyone on the trauma team agreed to bring something. Thanksgiving is my favorite holiday, I was sorely missing the crackle of the fireplace, the family in-jokes, Mom's dressing, and my sister's mac and cheese, but I was thankful for anything to mark the occasion and to break up the monotony of cafeteria food. My trauma chief, George, was from eastern Europe. With fast fingers, heavy steps, and weary eyes, he never raised his voice and never seemed to leave the hospital. His ham would be the centerpiece.

My contribution that Thanksgiving was a pale shrimp cocktail tray from Jewel grocery store. Those skinny, watery shrimps waited in the surgery lounge refrigerator for our planned 4 P.M. dinner, but when dinnertime came, we were all still in the trauma bay working up a fairly mundane car accident. George left to warm up the ham while I went with the patient to the CT scanner. As soon as his results were negative, I headed to the lounge for dinner. There was no turkey and no greens, but we found things to laugh about, and the ham with the Hawaiian sweet rolls was legit. Whether a Labor Day BBQ in the ambulance bay or Christmas Eve potlucks, working on a holiday meant a spread—until today. COVID keeps us from eating together. Not even a benefactor's "Hero" meal. This year, Fourth of July meals are solo affairs.

"Code Yellow, Level Two in five minutes." My team assembled again in the trauma bay to receive a man with blood-stained gauze wrapped around his entire face. By paramedic report, he's a twenty-nine-year-old, 200-pound Black man—and blind. He has been hit with a metal rod a number of times. Sitting upright in the gurney in blood-stained jeans and a T-shirt, his mouth and nose are exposed through the gauze, and he's using enough medical terminology to let us know that he's clear-headed and either well educated or someone who has experienced a lot of health care or both.

"As soon as they hit me, my left eye went black," he says.

"Wait, sir, they said you were blind already."

"I'm legally blind because I cannot see out of my right eye, but I could see 20/300 out of my left. Now that's dark."

When we unwrap his gauze, he's got a large bloody laceration on his scalp, another over his right eye, another on his back, and his left eye is swollen shut. "When they hit me, I saw stars, and then everything went dim." Trying to open the eye hurts too much to try more than once, and blood trickles down his face from the lacerations. We summon ophthalmology to the trauma bay and send him to the CT scan for images of his brain and eye socket while we await their arrival.

"Fuck this bullshit, leave me alone!" I hear from beyond the closed doors of the trauma bay. With these injured patients stabilized and in CT, I step out and toward the noise but safely behind the charge nurse's desk. Six police officers and two paramedics escort a small and furious woman from the ambulance bay into the hallway in front of the desk. She's not wearing pants or shoes and the top of her head is bald, pink and raw, likely from pulling out her own hair. The rest of her head is wreathed by wisps of gray hair. She appears to be having a psychotic break. She looks like she would be on the verge of running out of the ward altogether if not for the formation of men around her.

"Don't touch me!" she seethes. And they don't. One paramedic gives a nod and hand gesture to the charge nurse that says, "Where do we take her?"

"C'mon, we're going to Room 22!" directs the charge nurse after searching the track board for space. I join the entourage of six police, two paramedics, two techs, and two nurses headed to the psychiatric room. At the center of it is this half-naked ball of fire.

Once in Room 22, the police escorts tell us she was in the street disrobing when somebody called 911.

"I'm here for my medication, and then I can go!" she yells. It's not clear if she's resisting or participating, but that's a sound plan.

"We can do that," I reply, now in Room 22 with her, but it isn't a simple conversation given her public undressing, hostile body language, and high volume. One shot of medication may not be enough. She may need a few days to stabilize.

"I need the bathroom," she says, and with that the entire entourage guides her from Room 22 across the hall to the toilet, which was designed expressly for psychiatric patients, without breakable or movable fixtures. One nurse gives her a cup for a urine sample. When she returns, a tech helps her get into a hospital gown, and her nurse prepares a shot of an antipsychotic medicine. The patient says she'll accept the injection but remains belligerent in tone, balancing opposition and collaboration.

"She can touch me, but not you and not you!" she says, pointing last at me, so I wait outside her room along with the police and the rest of the team. There's no point escalating or bullying when we can do this easily by working with her. She promptly calms down when only one nurse and one tech are in the room. After her shot, we turn off the lights so she can sleep as the medication takes its effect. We'll come back after the drugs have blunted her psychosis.

Before the day is over I see two patients with COVID—both of whom had come in for other reasons—but not one person with a gunshot wound. As I wrap up and sign out, the trauma alert freezes me again: "Level 1 trauma, ten minutes." Gunshot to the chest. But not for me.

By Monday, after a three-day span, eighty people will have been shot in Chicago, and I won't have seen a single one. Gun violence is the inverse of COVID. People who are safe feel threatened, and people who are threatened do everything in their power to stay safe. At this point the familiarity and sometimes subtle symptoms of COVID leave me unfazed, but even though violence is as common, when I end up in the room with a gunshot victim, the gruesome wounds capture my subconscious. But not today. Today the guns exploded behind me and around me but failed to go off right in front of my face. Violence, COVID, and the holiday were present all shift, each hiding and masquerading in its own way.

9

Dear Dania,

We worked together in your first week as a doctor. It was July 4, and the ER swirled around you during a violent period of the year. As patient volume began to rebound from its COVID lows, the city's violence was peaking. You had new systems to learn and colleagues to meet. Everything was new. One of your first patients was an older gentleman with a mysterious and complicated condition that caused his hand to swell. We sorted through a treatment plan, but the test he needed wasn't available because of the holiday. Without that test, you became frustrated by your patient's clinical uncertainty and the lack of available options. Soon you'll see more of this: waiting rooms crammed with people waiting eight or ten hours before they see you, and tests and specialists just beyond their reach. You might think that if you just work faster and harder, you'll be able see everyone who waits, cajole specialists to care for your patients, and maneuver cases toward more timely testing. Sometimes you can, but these issues will usually remain beyond your control. While you didn't know it at the time, today you glimpsed the way money shapes our clinical systems. I know medical school teaches you very little about how money flows in health care, but maybe I can help you understand why your patient couldn't get his ultrasound. It was not because you weren't working hard enough.

I don't have to tell you this, but money shapes America, and health care is not separate from its influence. In fact, the health-care industry is a cornerstone of the American economy. It is the largest employer in the country. From the engineers who keep our hospital in good shape to the laboratory technicians in the companies that make medications, more than twenty million American workers are employed in health care. In many smaller towns, health care is the economic engine that has replaced factory work. As our economy booms and recedes, people continue to use the system, and the system keeps growing. At this point, about one in eight Americans works in the field. All these people, along with the drugs and technologies that treat illness, cost a lot. In 2018 we spent $1.2 trillion on hospitals, $726 billion on doctors, and $335 billion on prescription drugs, which still only accounted for 62 percent of the $3.6 trillion spent on health care. Taken together, health care makes up 17 percent of all the goods and services America produces in a year. This mountain of money is equal to each American spending $11,172 per person every year.

We know that those health-care expenditures are not evenly distributed. While most people account for very little of this outlay, a few people spend millions of dollars, mostly at the beginning and end of life. Costly and heroic interventions give us more hours or years at the end of our lives, and expensive technologies save preemies as early as twenty-four weeks. In between, most people spend very little on their health care except for the occasional accident, illness, preventive care, or pregnancy. When people come to you in the ER, the treatments you deliver are pricey. Your patient needed an ultrasound of his arm to look for a blood clot. It's a special technology guided by a trained technician and interpreted by a radiologist. Costing between $200 and $1,000, depending on where it's performed, it was unavailable to your patient on the holiday.

Whether or not your patient opens their pocket, hospitals have bills. Gauze and needles must be purchased, nurses deserve salaries, and expensive equipment like ventilators wears out and must be replaced—health care has costs. A visit to the ER averages $1,300, each night in the ICU is about $4,000, and the average stay in the hospital for COVID-19 is $73,000. Miraculous new cancer therapies, like chimeric antigen receptor T cells, cost about $475,000 for a course, and a dose of remdesivir to treat COVID-19 is $3,000. When you ordered that ultrasound, you were directing technology that is the fruit of decades of research and development. The hands that perform the study and the eyes that interpret the result have trained for years. And the prices result from sophisticated modeling designed to maximize return. Your medical training directs a plan to diagnose and treat your patient's swollen arm. Behind the scenes you've generated thousands of dollars in charges.

At those steep prices, nobody can afford these lifesaving therapies on their own. When we face defining health challenges, like when parents confront their child's leukemia or when a woman battles breast cancer in the prime of her life, prices rarely define our decisions. They are generally driven by a search for relief, trust, and cure. Unlike expensive car repairs or house renovations, where people have the time and information to shop for the right selection at the right cost, in health care it is difficult to search for bargains when we're sick, afraid, and fighting for our lives. Who wants to negotiate when your baby's life is in the balance? Even if patients wanted to compare charges, the prices of these therapies are hidden and difficult to assess at the time services are delivered. The fact is, everyone will fall sick and require care that costs more money than they have. To understand which of your patients receive more and which less, which services are easily accessed and which are difficult to find—like the ultrasound for your patient—we must consider how we pay for these valuable but costly services.

Today's health care is only possible because we share those exorbitant costs. Whether public or private, we pool resources and spread risk across a large population through systems of health insurance. Private health insurance was born during World War II. As the country manufactured war supplies, federally imposed wage controls barred employers from raising pay to recruit workers. When the War Labor Board declared that fringe benefits, like health insurance, did not count as income, employers responded by offering health-care coverage that has since evolved over the decades. Public health insurance came decades later, during the social changes of the Sixties. In 1965 Americans made a health commitment to one another by launching Medicare and Medicaid. Those public insurance plans cover health care for our elders and our low-income citizens, respectively. The Affordable Care Act improved private health insurance and expanded public insurance in 2010.

You will serve people with all three of these insurances in our ED. Many of your patients have Medicaid, some have Medicare, but our hospital values the patients who have private insurance the most.

Most working Americans and their families are sheltered from high health-care prices by private health insurance—but not your patient. These plans are usually linked to patients' jobs, and in 2019 they cov-

ered about 160 million Americans. Employers choose among private
insurance companies to offer their employees the cheapest and most
expansive coverage. Insurance companies compete to offer the best
benefits at a lower cost by negotiating discounts with doctors and
hospitals. On the other side of that negotiation, hospitals and doctors
want to be paid as much as possible for as many patients as they can
handle. Health-care providers with coveted services and strong repu-
tations can command higher fees, while prominent large health insurance companies can direct a lot of people to specific providers and
demand discounts in exchange for the volume. For example, Insurer
A may agree to pay 75 percent of the charges requested by a hospital, a discount of 25 percent. For a hospitalization resulting in $20,000
in charges, the hospital would receive a $15,000 payment for a pa-
tient covered by Insurer A. A different insurer, Insurer B, might have
more members and direct more people to the hospital. They might
negotiate a steeper discount and agree to pay 60 percent of billed
charges. They would pay $12,000 for that same $20,000 hospital bill.
Even at those discounts, hospitals like ours yield a surplus when serving privately insured patients, and they work hard to ensure that those
patients return for more care.

Your patient was covered by public insurance. These longstanding
government programs are the primary insurance for 139 million Americans, including most seniors, low-income children, people on dialysis, and those in nursing homes. Medicare is the federal insurance
program for elders and certain disabled individuals, and it protected
around 61 million people in 2019. Medicaid, which is administered by
the states and is funded jointly with the federal government, covers
about 75 million low-income adults and children. CHIP, also a federal/
state partnership, serves certain children and families who do not qual-
ify for Medicaid but who cannot afford private coverage; it reaches

about 6 million people. I keep these straight in my head by remembering that we *care* for the elderly: Medi*care*. And we *aid* the poor: Med-
ic*aid*. These programs were put in place and improved over time to
serve as America's health-care safety net. Since most of your patients
are older or poorer, one of these two insurance plans covers almost
all of the people in our ED.

Medicare protected your patient and serves as the economic foundation for most hospitals. Older people and those with disabilities use
more health care than younger people, filling hospital beds and physician schedules. This volume, along with central planning by the federal government, allows Medicare to set payment rates and define
conditions hospitals must meet in order to participate. For example,
Medicare funds hospitals to train resident physicians, and so the lion's share of your salary and benefits comes from the federal government. Plus, in 1966, Medicare drove the racial integration of thousands
of waiting rooms, hospital floors, and physician practices by making
payments to health-care providers conditional on desegregation.
Given this market power, Medicare pays about half what private insurers compensate for the same services. If Medicare is charged
$20,000 for that same hypothetical hospitalization that private insur-
ance companies reimbursed at $15,000 or $12,000, it will pay between $6,000 and $7,000.

Here on the South Side, a large portion of your patients have
Medicaid. It was instituted in 1965 by the same Congress that passed
Medicare. By combining federal and state dollars, Medicaid is the
largest source of health care for people with limited income. It also
offers benefits not covered by Medicare, including nursing home care
and personal care services. Medicaid is often the largest single com-
ponent of a state's budget; it makes up more than 27 percent of the
Illinois budget. Each state chooses whether or not to participate and

who is eligible for its program. That flexibility extends to the payment structure for doctors and hospitals; in general Medicaid pays providers the least of all insurers. Illinois Medicaid pays 61 cents for every dollar that Medicare pays. For that same $20,000 hospital charge I mentioned a minute ago, Medicaid pays about $4,500. That low reimbursement and the unusually slow payment means fewer skilled and enthusiastic doctors and hospitals accept patients with Medicaid.

Some of your patients have no insurance at all. Uninsured people find themselves trapped without the protection of pooled risk and pooled costs. Seven in ten of the 28 million uninsured have at least one full-time worker in the house—just not someone with one of the good jobs that offer insurance. The ACA lowered this number from 47 million in 2010, and thank goodness. People without insurance do not have the benefit of negotiated payment rates, nor the power of government, and as a result they face the full price of this expensive care. If an uninsured person, the person with the least ability to pay, has that same $20,000 hospital stay, they are charged the full $20,000.

If these uninsured patients receive care from one of the nonprofit hospitals (56 percent of the total), they may receive an automatic discount or have their bills dismissed entirely. Nonprofit hospitals are required to offer an ill-defined "community benefit" in exchange for tax avoidance. But forgiving bills is optional, and the uninsured may not be assisted at all. In fact, the total amount of uncompensated care provided by large nonprofit hospitals is generally less than 2 percent of total revenue. Often after a hospitalization, people without insurance are billed and then hounded to pay their debt. These bills quickly lead to garnished wages, a lifetime of medical debt, or bankruptcy. Among wealthy nations, these are unique conditions and add financial insult to physical injury.

It is difficult for your patients to stay healthy if they're uninsured, and even harder for them to get well once they fall ill. Doctors and hospitals that avoid Medicaid patients do even more to stay away from people who cannot pay for care. They discourage them with long wait times and advance payment requirements or simply send them to public providers if they can get away with it. In 2018 one in five uninsured adults was unable to get needed medical care due to cost. They were also less likely than those with insurance to receive preventive care and services for major health conditions and chronic diseases. As a result, people without health coverage are less likely than those with insurance to have regular outpatient care, and they are more likely to be hospitalized for avoidable health problems and to experience declines in their overall health. When they are hospitalized, uninsured people receive fewer diagnostic and therapeutic services and also have higher mortality rates than those with insurance.

Segregation magnifies the health-care challenges of your patients. Black folks, who comprise most of your patients, are less likely to have desirable private insurance than white people, and they are 50 percent more likely than white people to be uninsured. A map of Chicago's racial segregation demonstrates how Chicago crowds Black folks into communities with high rates of Medicaid or with no health insurance at all. Here on the South Side, in nearby Englewood 12.3 percent are uninsured, while only 2.5 percent are uninsured in the North Side's Lincoln Park. These geographic differences in a community's ability to pay for health care mean that whole neighborhoods on the South Side lack health outlets. A map of Chicago's segregation also is a map of health-care providers, with doctors and hospitals concentrated on the whiter North Side.

The way providers on the South Side respond to the concentration of patients who cannot pay them high rates is by providing fewer services. Sometimes they restrict access to specialized care and technologies, as in the case of the ultrasound for your patient. Others simply close during the off-hours when hardworking folks are able to seek care. The few outlets that do offer comprehensive services have trouble meeting the community's outsized needs. For these reasons and others, most of your patients face long waits for necessary care. In contrast, on the much wealthier and whiter North Side, the large numbers of privately insured patients mean there are more places to get care, and providers work hard to serve and recruit these patients. Following the lead of luxury hotels, medical centers create expensive ad campaigns that tout exclusive experiences with concierges, sweeping views, and gourmet food to attract insured patients. Your patient's inability to get an ultrasound on the holiday is typical of the constrained services offered in systems that treat large numbers of Medicaid and uninsured patients. Meanwhile, North Side hospitals of the same size are more likely to have 24/7 access to these resources.

Heath care where most of the patients are uninsured or on public insurance looks very different than it does in places where most people are insured. In the first case, wait times are long, specialists are few, nurses are scarce and often burned out, time with the doctor is short, testing and treatments are delayed, facilities are in disrepair, and amenities like soft blankets and pillows are absent. These healthcare settings struggle to care for the volume of people who need help and yet they often have back doors or other special access so prestigious, wealthy, or connected individuals do not face austere conditions. Conversely, clinical care where most people have insurance means no waiting, clean and pleasant facilities, prompt testing and treatment, receptive specialists, plenty of nurses, courteous and doting providers, and feedback loops to ensure services improve year-over-year. In both cases, the systems are predictable managerial responses to the payment they receive from their average patient. Whether or not any individual has insurance means less than whether their fellow patients have insurance.

In the course of your training, you will see this in detail. You'll have firsthand experience with people crowded forty or fifty deep in our waiting room. You'll observe when some of your patients are referred to public hospitals for follow-up with a specialist. You'll notice that sometimes elective care for the wealthy is prioritized at the expense of emergency care for the poor. At times you'll see specialists determine their treatment plan based on a patient's insurance. You'll notice how insured patients in our own facility are occasionally escorted past barricades to receive prompt care, taking advantage of the surplus created by withholding and delaying care for your everyday ER patients. You'll also rotate through hospitals that serve mostly privately insured patients, where almost every bed has a view and consultants consistently say "yes." Over time, you'll witness people without sources of regular health care being forced to use the Emergency Department for minor problems, and obstacles forcing them to wait until small issues grow to true emergencies. If you pay attention, you'll see that this pattern stratifies your patients by their race.

This biased apportionment has been exacerbated by COVID-19. The initial distributions of the $175 billion made available by the Coronavirus Aid, Relief, and Economic Security (CARES) Act showered the hospitals with the highest share of private insurance revenue with twice as much funding as the hospitals with the lowest share. Providers who care for privately insured patients got twice the relief of providers who serve those on Medicaid and without insurance. Hospitals and doctors who serve Medicaid patients, the very providers with the sickest patients and whose patients had the least ability to pay, had to wait weeks before landing economic relief.

To some, this seems a fair reward to those who have earned their privileges. To accept this, we must reconcile the inequity of channeling shared riches to those who already have the most. Our taxes support residency training via Medicare and discovery via the NIH, and our nonprofit medical centers enjoy tax-protected property and revenue. Black folks and white folks, rich and poor alike, support medical institutions, training, and technology with their tax dollars, and then these collective investments are heaped in the service of the wealthy and the disproportionately white. Health care is the one setting where our best natures, led by fact and science, should prevail over greed and bias in the service of humanity. This is not what I've found. The truth is the American health-care system, like all American systems, segregates, then drains resources and vitality from the Black and poor and fortifies the rich and white. Consistent with the stated values of market capitalism, our health-care system creates winners and losers—and the losers pay with their lives.

The fact is, your patients have few options. There are not many health-care outlets available to them, and they cannot shop around because they're often too sick to take the time and too poor to be accepted by many providers. For some of them, you are all they have. Once they come to you, the resources you can offer them are controlled. One of the key reasons for this is that financial incentives direct health-care assets away from those who have the least. Do you think that's fair? Are you happy with the care you offered your patient? But what if you believe that all of us are valuable and that value has nothing to do with whether you have insurance or not? And what if you believe there can be no losers when our precious health is at stake?

I hope you believe those things. And I hope that you keep an eye on the bigger picture as you care for your patients. As you train, not only will you learn how to diagnose and treat, you'll ascertain how to advocate and maneuver. You'll learn the administrative work-arounds that provide wealthy patients prompt and superb care. And I hope you use those same tactics to deliver needed services to all your patients. In fact, I hope you'll persist, demand, and advocate for every patient, whether they're rich or poor, Black or white, insured or not—they all deserve that. But when you fail, remember that this is bigger than you and even bigger than your hospital. This is as big as America.

Onward,

tlf

10

AUGUST 2020

RICHARD STRIDES OVER TO my station in a crisp white shirt and gray slacks tailored to his build.* He rarely wears scrubs like everyone else, preferring to flaunt his fashion sense. He stays clean by delegating, by avoiding the messy parts of our job. Richard is in his seventies, years past the age most people retire. In the Emergency Department's darkest days, after consecutive section heads resigned, he raised his hand to lead and stayed at the helm a couple of years. Although we have a twenty-year relationship, his decisions in that period led to years in which we didn't speak. Now we're cordial. Despite a bum leg and special shoe, he still has a bounce in his stride and a playful tone: "How was your shift, Tom?" he asks. From behind my N95, my response is curt and raspy from dehydration: "I'm all right."

---

* Richard is a pseudonym signaling a composite character.

Richard is here to relieve me at 2:30 P.M., and not a moment too soon. It's been a conference day for residents, who, liberated from their clinical duty, attended Zoom lectures from 7 A.M. to about 1 P.M. I've been left on my own for the past eight hours. In a normal shift, the residents shield me from the convoluted processes of ordering radiology and the interminable calls to get a patient admitted. Today all that work was mine. I was out of practice, so it took me forever to remember how to get stuff done. I'd meet and examine a patient and quickly decide on a diagnostic pathway, but get stuck for a half hour or more trying to figure out the minutiae. I nagged the nurses with questions. The bed desk called multiple times to tell me I was filling out the admission forms wrong, and the pharmacists helped me adjust the way I was entering antibiotic doses. After eight hours of flailing, Richard's relief was welcome.

Richard asks again, "Are you well?" and extends his hand for a shake.

I offer an elbow bump and wearily repeat, "I'm all right. I'm ready for COVID to be over. I miss traveling."

And with that opening, he takes off on a monologue. He lets me know that after training generations of doctors for more than thirty years, he's financially secure, a septuagenarian, and now alone. He divulges that his wife is in California and won't see him as long as he continues to take care of patients—the COVID risk is just too high. Her absence has left him with more time to spend with TV pundits.

"We have to get these schools open," Richard says gravely. I recognize this talking point from chatter on the web. I'm chagrined but not surprised to hear this from him.

After a long pause and a deep sigh, I ask, "How can we do that safely with the virus circulating at such high rates? We still see cases every day." I feel my jaw clenching.

"It will be fine! Like a chicken pox party. Everyone will get sick, and then they'll be immune." I'm sure my scowl is hidden by the mask, but my disgust must have shown up in my eye roll or some other bit of body language. Richard finishes with more encouragement: "Smile more. Be optimistic." A nurse who has been listening touches my hand and murmurs, "Get out of here as fast as you can."

Has Richard thought this through? Getting kids back in school is a critical goal, but is this proposal a conspiracy theory or is it a sound solution based in epidemiology and modeling? It seems kids in school will lead to infections that they'll bring home to their families, infecting school workers and bus drivers along the way. While not so dangerous in kids, those infections will kill adults and people with chronic illness. Is that chain of transmission the whole point? Is this just a variation on the "herd immunity" strategy that would result in 1.2 million dead? Why does he choose "optimism" and ignore the sick people just a few feet away? "Chicken pox party" makes for a compelling meme, but we stopped having those thirty years ago, when the varicella shot became widespread. What's the relevance of just-so stories from a bygone era when we're facing a virus we've never seen before? Our country's response is fraught with cynicism and misinformation—even the CDC has been corrupted—and we're facing a virus we've never seen before. We can't ever be certain of the right path forward, and now we have no reliable guide to hack a clear path through this tangle. Maybe Richard knows something I don't, but I doubt it.

On my walk to the car, the dissonance of my conversation with Richard sends me spiraling back to thoughts of a patient I saw a few hours before. Ambulance 38 brought a very sick seventy-year-old man to the infamous Room 41, the negative pressure room originally created to deal with Ebola. Mr. Thornton had been walking up a flight of stairs when his chest tightened and his breath became short. After calling 911 he sat down and felt like he was going to pass out. He held on, and in the ambulance they performed an EKG that showed he was having a heart attack. The nurse who received the call activated the cardiac catheterization lab in order to prepare the cardiology team for his arrival. When the paramedics transferred him from their stretcher to our bed, he was ashen and breathing so fast that he could speak only in one- or two-word bursts. His blood pressure was low, and his heart rate was high.

I met them in the room with a team of nurses. In concert one performed a confirmatory EKG, another started an IV, and a third readied medications that deactivate platelets, thinning the blood. "Sir, it looks like you're having a heart attack," I said. "That means there's a blockage in a blood vessel that brings oxygen to your heart. The cardiology team is on their way to help. They'll take you upstairs, put a large needle in a vessel in your groin, fish a catheter up to your heart and use a tiny balloon to erect a metal cage in order to open that artery. This procedure is called a coronary angioplasty." Mr. Thornton was shirtless, with visible ribs heaving with each breath. Rather than lying back, he was perched with his legs swung over the side of the gurney and his hands on his knees, his lips pursed. "Okay, Doc. . . . I'm . . . ready."

Fifteen minutes after he arrived, the cardiologists were nowhere to be found. Fifteen minutes doesn't sound like a long time, but I felt like I was watching a man being held underwater. With each wasted minute killing more of his heart muscle, I called the hospital operator to page the cath lab again. After another ten minutes the cardiology fellow, Dr. Carry, arrived. He was bespectacled and balding in a crisp white coat. He looked as old as me, although I suspected I had a decade on him. His job, in his final year of training, is to prepare and accompany the patient to the cath lab, where the attending will be waiting to treat the blocked artery. He was jolted by the patient's labored breathing.

"Oh boy, he's sick," he says. "Maybe we should intubate him."

"No! He's talking, coherent, and engaged. His breathing will resolve when you open that artery."

"But if we put him on the ventilator, the door-to-balloon clock stops." The standard of care for heart attacks is to open the blocked vessel with the balloon-initiated stent less than ninety minutes after a patient arrives at the hospital—we call that the door-to-balloon time. The more quickly and aggressively we move, the better the outcome. However, putting someone on a ventilator artificially stops the clock. By putting him on a ventilator, we would both delay the stenting and remove the time pressure for the cardiology team to open the artery. We needed folks accountable to the clock, rushing to save his heart and his life, not searching for stopgaps.

"No. Take him up. He needs to be in the cath lab. Is your team ready?"

Still shaky, Dr. Carry wondered whether we should get a CT of his chest to make sure he didn't have an aortic dissection.

"Can't you find that in the cath lab?" I ask. I knew Dr. Carry was worried that this might be a rare disorder rather than a common heart attack. It is reassuring to acquire exhaustive information before decisive action, but in an emergency, with speed defining life and death, sometimes we must leap from the comfort of certainty and proceed. The standard of care was clear, and when we do this by the book, we give patients the best chance at survival. We could not know how long the patient could hold on, and the sense that we were dithering while someone dies in front of us was excruciating. Nevertheless, Dr. Carry dawdled another twenty minutes debating the critical intervention before he finally departed with Mr. Thornton. Within minutes after they'd left, the overhead paging system called "Dr. Cart" to the cath lab, summoning the cardiac arrest team to resuscitate our patient. His heart stopped in the cath lab.

In the moment, I didn't have time to wonder whether I did the right thing. But here in the car, the second guesses come to life. Why didn't he follow the protocol? Could I have made stronger demands? Should I have intubated the patient rather than debate? Why didn't I go over the fellow's head and call the attending cardiologist directly? Maybe there wasn't a better answer, but I have seen more aggressive care for critical cases like this. The lifesaving intervention did not have to be delayed. For some patients, the hospital works like a well-oiled machine.

Weeks ago, I tended to the board chairman of a large organization who was having a stomachache. She was ushered right in and didn't spend any time in the waiting room. Before I had a chance to enter her room my phone buzzed with calls from my boss, her boss, and the dean to ensure I knew a VIP was in the ED. The charge nurse swung by to prompt me to meet the executive in Room 38. The banner of her electronic medical record was gold rather than the normal blue.

In contrast to our usual slow process, that day there were no impediments to care, no debates, no delays. The Emergency Department was a whir of activity and efficiency: lab tests returned in moments, warm blankets were procured, and pain medications were quickly dispensed. An abdominal CT was performed in minutes, and the patient was found to have a life-threatening aortic aneurysm right where it passed by her stomach. Soon graying and stooped attending anesthesiologists, interventional radiologists, and vascular surgeons came to the Emergency Department to meet the VIP. Convening to discuss next steps, surgery staging, and her post-surgical plan, these doctors commented on the spaciousness of the now two-year-old ED. They'd never been down here before.

I've seen what is possible. Sometimes the right resources are all around us. We clear away inefficiency and delay, and great care proceeds without hesitation. But today my patient languished. During the peak of COVID, processes were aligned, and service for everyone resembled VIP care. Those days are over. My patient wasn't important enough—he was just a man. He didn't have a platform or an influential social circle, and I guess that made the difference. Obstacles, delay, and disorganization may have cost him his life. But maybe he was going to die no matter what.

A warm breeze fills the car and breaks my hospital-air-conditioned chill. On Garfield Boulevard I pass an abandoned bread factory on my way to the expressway. When I was a kid that factory perfumed the summer air with a nourishing aroma that made me feel hopeful. It's been derelict for two decades now. I realize my younger colleagues never knew the South Side when the breeze smelled like optimism. Today I worked with two of them, both Black. Olga has beautiful curly hair and the confidence that comes from quiet brilliance. Q comes from the South Side, wears Air Force 1s, and has a relationship with every staff member. We spend an hour speculating whether the section head's impending retirement presents a window for change. The ongoing protests sparked by police killing Black men has created a moment for what the hospital calls "diversity and inclusion." Maybe this time we will see more than words and gestures.

At the intersection where I hop on the Dan Ryan, I swerve to avoid debris from an earlier collision. All year long, this intersection is littered with pieces of cars. As soon as wreckage from one accident is moved aside, another impact sprays more glass and metal on the pavement. After I get home, I take a nap, then I watch the setting sun's oranges fade into an ombré of blues and indigos. Fall is coming. As streetlights blink to life, their reflections on the glassy buildings dress the city in sequins. This year, the imminent dusk of autumn is accented by flashing lights on the snowplow trucks that quietly line up on the expressway. At the top of the hour, with a choreographed synchrony, they block the downtown exits, obstructing protestors' access to the business district.

As the city raged with protests in the wake of George Floyd's death, I cared for the demonstrators who had been beaten and pepper-sprayed. But raised bridges and blocked exits quieted my neighborhood. For a city ablaze, there were no protests near me, no looting, and no sign of unrest. But I didn't escape the siege of this summer. On weekends the chill of loneliness descended and couldn't be warmed in the usual ways. COVID meant I couldn't get on a plane, go for dinner, or hug my family. Movie theaters and museums remained closed. And safe outdoor walks with my niece, park bench cocktails with friends, and Sunday family picnics occurred at the whim of the police. Usually autumn's cooler temperatures and the return to school mark the end of Killing Season. This year, when people have nothing to do, I'm not sure that will happen.

When I arrive at the ED the next day, the rooms are mostly empty. I see the lead resident on duty, mask askew and bags under her eyes, clearly frazzled and tired. I don't recognize her, so I move closer and get a look at her ID. Her name is Susan. I don't know many of the second-year residents—in their first year they spend only a couple months in the ED, and their faces have been covered since March. I cannot pick her or many of her colleagues out of a crowd. When I ask how she's doing, she tells me that she's frustrated by the patient in Room 15.

Ms. Pierce in Room 15 has a minor problem, painful plantar fasciitis affecting the sole of her foot. This inflamed connective tissue emits shocks of intense pain each time she steps on the foot. Skimming the chart informs me that the patient has been bothered by this for the past year and has tried pills and injections to soothe the pain. Yesterday she was in the Emergency Department and experienced some relief from a series of pills, but returned today. When I arrive, she's already been in the ED eight hours. Now that I'm taking over her care, Susan and I need to figure out what we can do differently.

"Susan, Room 15 is complicated, isn't she? What's her plan?"

"We just can't make her happy! We've given her two shots,

she's had an ultrasound to check for a blood clot, and we scheduled an MRI for Tuesday. I just got off the phone with the podiatrist. He won't come see her because she has an appointment
coming up. And she won't go home, she wants to stay."

Susan's voice is tense. She just wants this case over with.

"Well," I ask, "what can I do? Maybe I can go talk to her? Get
a better understanding?" Susan crosses her arms, and her eyes
avert.

"You've done everything right, gone above and beyond," I
say. "It seems like some of what's going on here is not medical.
When people are unhappy, things get jammed. It's even more
sticky when they feel frustrated, tired, or sad."

Some of my talk is thinking of a strategy out loud, but the
rest is teaching Susan to see this situation in a bigger context. If
I understand what is unsaid, we might find a resolution. And
with that I walk into the room.

Ms. Pierce is a small woman with the hint of a West African
accent. She has long braids, blue at their tips. When I introduce
myself and sit down, she avoids eye contact.

"Hey, I'm Dr. Fisher. I'm the supervisor. I'm just coming on
shift and want to meet you. I heard you have pain in the bottom
of your foot, and it's been there for a long time."

"Yes! And nobody wants to do anything!"

"Well, I understand you've gotten steroid shots in the past,
but your podiatrist won't give you another one until you've had
an MRI."

"That's what he keeps telling me. But every time I schedule
the MRI, I have to work."

"That must be frustrating," I respond. Her nose and mouth

are covered by a mask, but I can see the deep furrow in her brow. Her hospital gown is neatly tied, and she's sitting on the gurney with her legs under a blanket.

Ms. Pierce tells me she hasn't been to work lately because her foot hurts too much. Even when she hangs the foot off the side of the bed, it still hurts. "I know you've tried a lot of medication," I say. "Have you tried Neurontin?"

"Yes! It doesn't work."

"Have you tried ibuprofen?"

"Yes! It doesn't work either, and I can't be on it long because it will damage my kidneys." Not everyone knows that ibuprofen is linked to kidney damage. That she has some insight into this suggests she is a health-care worker.

So I ask, "Do you work in a hospital?"

She replies, "I do. I'm a phlebotomist. I see all kinds of bullshit admitted to my hospital, but for some reason you people don't want to admit me for my foot. Just give me pain medicines and let me stay overnight. Do something!"

"Which hospital do you work at?" I ask, hoping to gather information about the bigger picture.

"Look! Stay out of my business! Just help me!"

I have lost her confidence by deflecting, so I regroup, focused on being honest and calm. I say, "I know what I'm going to say might feel frustrating, but staying overnight may not be useful. Most of the things that we can do for you here, you can do at home."

I remain seated the whole time. When patients are exasperated and angry, it's easy to be drawn into their tension. Sitting helps me stay calm and thoughtful about what's being said and also attuned to what's behind the words. With few options and with time pressure, there's every incentive to simply go through the motions. Sitting forces me to be intentional.

"The benefit of home is that you're safer from COVID and hospital injuries."

"But why can't I just stay?"

"Okay. So let me ask: can the team give you more shots in your foot like the ones we gave you?"

"No!"

"Okay. Then are you interested in physical therapy?" I know it's an empty promise on the weekend, but I want to understand what she is hoping for.

"I've tried it. It doesn't work. I know that's not happening anyway, it's the weekend," she replies. With that she looks at me for the first time. Directly into my eyes. I look back. She's crying. This is where we are.

She breaks into tears over and over again as we continue talking. She grits her teeth and demands to be admitted and then resolves to go home with the understanding that nothing is going to happen in the hospital over the weekend. Back and forth, back and forth. A few years ago, I'd have offered narcotics, but now we know opiates addict and kill people with chronic pain. I try to avoid them when I can. Here I've got no good remedies, and I let her know that.

"I'm frustrated that I don't have any good answers for your suffering. I can tell that you're even more discouraged than I am. We could try morphine, but that could cause more problems." Aligning with her against the problem has done nothing to improve her situation—or her mood.

She quietly sobs and looks to the ceiling. She tells me about a home remedy her husband rubs on her foot—but not even that is working now. She's tried so many things. She's tired. I ask, "Have you been depressed over this?" Her eyes lock into mine again. Now they're red. With tears streaming she says, "Leave me alone. Just help me."

She's probably not going to open up further. We all grow trust at our own pace.

"Ms. Pierce, what can I do? You don't want another shot, you don't want these medications because they don't work, you don't want to go home, you don't want to sit here doing nothing all weekend. What should we try? Can I get you some crutches?" She shakes her head, still crying, as though there's something obvious that I just haven't grasped. Finally, she says, "Fine. Let's do it." But clearly, it's not fine.

"Okay, I'll get those crutches, and let's try a few medications to see if they help."

Ten hours into her stay, I have nothing left for her, and already I'm tired. She's right—we do admit a bunch of bullshit. While admitting her will expose her to a small risk of COVID and is unlikely to help her, I'm also not willing to kick her out.

When I sit down in front of a computer to document this quagmire, a woman on a motorized wheelchair rolls herself into Room 13. I hear her yelling and crying, so I hop up out of my chair, adjust my mask, and walk around the desk to see what's going on. She's on FaceTime with her mask looped under her chin, screaming into her phone. Susan and Nurse Amy join me and listen to her side of the conversation.

"How dare you do this to me!" she hollers. "I can't believe I let you hurt me! You're going to pay for this! I'm going to call the police!" I assume it's an intimate partner issue and ask Amy to see if Frankie, the social worker, can help.

After I return to my desk and finish my notes on Ms. Pierce, Susan tells me that the yelling patient is named Ms. Floyd. She was actually on the phone with her primary-care doctor. It turns out Ms. Floyd has a severe kidney injury caused by a new medication that her primary-care doctor prescribed for her congestive heart failure. The medication was added two weeks ago, and in yesterday's routine blood draw, they noted her kidney problem. In fixing one problem they caused another. Ms. Floyd was called at home with the results and was told to come directly to the Emergency Department.

She has calmed down by the time I go to see her. I meet with her as she sits on the gurney, fully dressed in a lavender and white striped shirt, a matching purple windbreaker, lavender leggings, and gym shoes of the same shade of purple. Her hands are balled up, and her face is fully hidden behind a surgical mask and dark sunglasses. With her purple motorized wheelchair sitting next to the bed, she sits fully erect, staring directly ahead. Her voice trembles when she speaks.

"I did not want to be here . . . ," she says.

"I can imagine," I say, pulling a chair over. Her chin is quivering. "What's going on?" I ask.

"I've been doing just fine at home trying to hide from this plague," she says. "My doctor gave me this new medication, and she destroyed my kidneys. This is not fair!" I can feel the rage vibrating inside her. She lifts her fists and settles them again on her lap. Her voice comes back even, the rage controlled. "I did not ask for this. I do not deserve this."

"You are absolutely right," I reply, trying to catch her gaze, but she refuses to look me in the eye. "I am so sorry that this is happening. What did they tell you?"

"Well, they said that I needed to come in and be admitted. But I do not *want* to come in here and catch COVID. I'll die from it. I have preexisting conditions. I've been sitting at home just fine with my husband and kids. We get along fine without any arguments! My three dogs get along fine! My cat gets along fine!"

"What are your dogs' names?" I inquire. I am still searching for a point of connection, something to remind her of home, of safety. Something to remind her that things aren't all bad.

"It doesn't matter, Doctor. I just want to go home and pet them."

"I got it. I want you to get better. You do not deserve this. And this is not jail, and I'm not the cops. You can always go home, and I'm happy to send you home if that's what you want."

She finally takes a look in my direction, but only so she can give me a side-eye. "It's not fair for you to tell me that it's my decision after my other doctor ordered me to come in."

She's right. "Well, ma'am, let me give you my recommendations. When somebody has kidney failure and heart failure, we need to give them fluids through an IV in order to rejuvenate their kidneys. But if we give them too much, it can back up into their lungs, making it hard to breathe. And as you know, once it's in your lungs it takes a long time to get it back out. That means it's very delicate, and it's very hard to get that right at home. My advice would be to admit you to the hospital so that we can do this right, revive your kidneys without causing your lungs to fill up with fluid. I know you just want to live your life, but now we're stuck with a reality you didn't choose."

She starts crying.

"I just wanna go home! I can't believe you all did this to me. I just want. To. Go. Home! And live my life." *You all?* I often forget, but once I am in scrubs and badged, I'm part of "you all."

"Ms. Floyd, I want the same for you. We are on the same side here. I just worry that if you go home, we won't be able to manage this, and if your kidneys fail you could end up on dialysis. Hooked up to a machine three days a week. That's also not living your life."

"You're going to kill me with this virus."

She doesn't know me. Doesn't know I give a fuck. Doesn't know she reminds me of my surly high school math teacher Ms. Cortez, who would threaten us with detention if we didn't sit down and be quiet. She'd always finish her reprimands with a note of intimidation: "That's not a threat. It's a promise." Ms. Cortez had rosy cheeks and bangs that looked like she rolled them neatly every night. When one of our classmates was shot, Ms. Cortez hugged us and cried.

Ms. Floyd's hands are clenched, and her face mask is wet with tears.

"I do not want to stay."

Her nurse comes in, and I make one last attempt: "This is your nurse, Emily. Would you mind if she starts an IV? You don't have to decide about anything else right now. Let's just take one step at a time."

It's dark when I finally leave the hospital. There are no windows in the ED, so when I arrive in daylight and depart in darkness, it feels like more than a single day has elapsed. After a frustrating shift, the humid night air provides no refreshment. Outside the ED, cars line both sides of the street, filling both the parking and no parking curbs. The car doors are open, hazards

on and music playing. People are everywhere. Their faces show
hard lines of grief and languid eyes full of worry. I walk right
down the middle of the street, as both sidewalks are crowded
with families and friends embracing, smoking Black & Milds, or
sipping something. Elders sit hunched in lawn chairs, elbows on
their knees and holding their heads, or leaned back looking to
the heavens. Most are awaiting information about family members who have been shot. COVID keeps us from allowing visitors, so they congregate outside. Working in the low-acuity
area, I avoided the "code yellow" alarms and the bloody trauma
bay, but nevertheless these evenings full of violence haunt the
entire community. It's so ubiquitous that I have deep gratitude
for the decades since someone close to me has been shot. Culture, statistics, and theories try to make sense out of this absur-
dity. But we are just chemistry and physics made sentient, on a
rock flying in the void of space. As much as I want to order our
existence, it's inexplicable. This is chaos.

11

Dear Richard,

You took over from me last shift. COVID has stressed us all and strained the rapport in our long relationship. Like all bonds that have spanned decades, ours has had ups and downs, periods of proximity and distance. I wouldn't be here if you hadn't taught me emergency medicine, helped me become chief resident all those years ago, and written strong letters to support my fellowships and grants. And then we hit a period over a decade ago that was so gloomy that it changed everything. That crucible reshaped my view of medicine, and those dark days of confrontation filled me with dread but also great clarity. It was early in my career and later in yours, but I remember it clearly. Do you?

In those days, heading to work felt like walking to the gallows—as the executioner, not the condemned. It was February 2009, and the Emergency Department was overcrowded, with wait times so long that a patient in the waiting area was once found slumped in a wheel-chair, cold and pulseless, dead before ever having been seen. The Great Recession laid off thousands in the community, and our hospi-tal, like hospitals around the country, followed suit by downsizing and closing inpatient beds. With fewer beds available to admitted ER pa-tients, people who were too sick to go home often waited in the ED more than twenty-four hours before they went to a room upstairs. The hospital's solution to these long delays for admission was to transfer languishing patients to nearby hospitals.

Do you remember the transfer process? The first step was when a doctor, one of us, secured the patient's consent. On February 12, 2009, one of our colleagues approached every patient who had been waiting for a bed longer than eighteen hours to offer them space at another hospital. He took notes on these relocation proffers and bound them in a log more than four sheets long. His first patient was a man born in 1916. No longer able to care for himself due to progres-sive weakness, he came to the Emergency Department looking for help. He refused transfer to a hospital three miles away, telling our colleague, "I'm too old. They have no way to visit me," meaning his family. Notes from the next woman showed that she was born in 1930 and needed antibiotics for an infected bedsore. She cautiously as-sented: "I guess I would go. But I don't know anything about that hospital." Sick with diabetes and a foot ulcer threatening an amputa-tion, a third patient, age seventy-four, responded, "I would not like to leave the university, but I would go if that was my only option. I don't know that neighborhood. I'm not comfortable going over there." My colleague even approached a seventy-six-year-old man delirious with chest pain. He replied, "I'd rather go home and talk to my maker than go to another hospital." We were trained to care for people in their weakest moments, but in 2009 our job was convincing bedridden people to go away. Do you remember that sickening, cowardly feeling in your belly when you asked an elderly person to go somewhere else? I do. I can't forget those days.

I was hired in 2006, just three years before these troubles. I was one of the first two Black attendings appointed to supervise care in the Emergency Department. While you did not hire me, your early support and faith in me pushed the university to create my position. I came on board just after the CEO of the Medical Center set forth his vision for the institution. In a medical journal, the CEO described a siege facing urban academic medical centers. He decried how medical centers like ours face the issues of declining NIH funding, reduced reimbursement, skyrocketing costs of malpractice, and rising numbers of poor people who cannot pay. The article outlined how serving "urban" populations poses an existential threat not only to academic medical centers but also to other providers in the community. In this framing, urban academic medical centers and community providers are in the wrong arrangement. Patients are wastefully served by the high-cost academic medical center's primary-care teams. And worse, by delivering primary care to an "urban" community, the Medical Center is performing the job of the community's essential providers. In the process it is taking away needed jobs and money from those safety-net, primary-care doctors. According to the article, the Medical Center's resources were better spent on complex care.

This plan did not speak to the austere conditions that confront the community providers, nor the deep investment necessary to build enough quality primary-care options in "urban neighborhoods." It was silent on how health care has evolved to serve the wealthy rather than those who are most in need. It also didn't identify the Medical Center's responsibilities to the South Side, given the rich benefits it receives from a huge public investment. But it did make clear that

poor neighborhood people are undesirable patients for an urban medical center and that their routine problems must be excluded from the
academic setting.

Given that the medical center cannot just pick up and move to
evade the blitz of the "urban" population, the article proposed a deft
sleight of hand: an urban academic medical center's true community
is not the neighborhood where it sits but all patients who need complicated treatments, no matter where they come from. With this refor-
mulation, the Medical Center had little responsibility to the sick people
who show up in the Emergency Department or to the local community
whose tax dollars support the Medical Center's exempt status. This
philosophy justified plans to reallocate hospital beds and close space
in the ER, where the "urban" population seeks basic care. Like medical centers around the country, our hospital would transfer out the
local patients who overflow and invest more in technology, advertis-
ing, and comforts to attract people from far away who have complicated medical needs.

It seems obvious now, Richard, but did you see how this road map
made health care conditional and charted plans for community exclusion over the next few years?

I joined the university medical center with great optimism. Here I
could effect change in the same community I grew up in. When I in-
terviewed, the hospital's leaders reinforced my hope as they described goals of better care for the poor and vulnerable who show up
to the ER every day. I could not wait to help them do just that. I spent
the first couple of years growing into my role, developing skills and
building a program to address chronic illness by creating partnerships
that linked community-organized support groups with the hospital's
resources, medications, and treatments. Then, two years after I was
hired, in 2008, risky financial instruments called collateralized debt

obligations (CDOs) led to a worldwide economic collapse. In response, the hospital accelerated its plans to abandon the neighborhood it stood in. My neighborhood.

Organizational emails from 2008 described how we would divert patients away from the ED to care elsewhere. Soon a task force was formed. We held meetings and generated a step-by-step, data-driven relocation process. Gantt charts, work plans, and a budget arranged the method whereby we would take sick people from our ED and deposit them somewhere else. The next step came soon after: inpatient hospital beds available to ER patients were reallocated to cancer and cardiac patients. Dressing it up with catchphrases like "distinction trumps volume," and "bed geography," the hospital embarked on a plan to exclude the South Side in favor of people who came from the North Side as well as far-off Wisconsin and Indiana.

You and my other mentors told me not to worry about those administrative plans. You framed the clogged ER and suffering patients as a distraction from my partnership programs. You and my other mentors reassured me that I had a very bright future if I just focused on building my research and intervention project. When you offered that advice, did you know that the tormented patients were people from my community, people I knew, both literally and figuratively? Do you remember when I shared how I struggled to reconcile planning programs for the future against the damage we're causing today — injury to the same people my research is trying to save? Ever the idealist, I wanted to believe you. I trusted that these were temporary plans, plans that leadership would scale back once they saw the harm they had caused. Good people would not stand behind poor-quality, discriminatory health care.

Then one day a child named Dontae Adams was mauled by a pit bull and came to the hospital. The *Chicago Tribune* wrote:

When a stray pit bull attacked 12-year-old Dontae Adams last August, tearing a chunk of the boy's upper lip from his face, his mother took him to the University of Chicago Medical Center. Instead of rushing Dontae into surgery, however, Angela Adams said, the hospital's staff began pressing her about insurance.

Adams said she demanded that the medical staff admit Dontae but that they refused. The emergency room staff gave Dontae a tetanus shot, a dose of morphine, prescriptions for antibiotics and Tylenol 3, and told Adams to "follow up with Cook County" in one week, according to medical center documents.

A child who had been disfigured by a dog was sent away because of insurance. Where was our oath to first do no harm? Where was the law that required that we care for all, regardless of ability to pay? Where were all those expressed desires to do better serving our community? Rejecting a mutilated child snuffed out my last glimmers of faith.

Then one day in early February 2009, the administration announced that they would shutter ICU beds and that many of the remaining hospital beds would be reallocated to special patients: Patients of Distinction. Patients of Distinction required specialists like oncology or cardiology and *also* had the ability to pay with private insurance. Those were not our typical ER patients. Giving beds to Patients of Distinction would further restrict the space available to admitted ER patients, worsening the overcrowding in our waiting room. The average wait time was already nine hours—that would certainly lengthen. Even worse, lingering patients would receive a cursory medical screening exam to satisfy the anti-dumping EMTALA law and then would be dispatched somewhere else. The woman with irregular bleeding who had finally arranged childcare and time off would be shuffled off to another clinic. Her neighbor would get no prescription for an itchy rash that had been keeping him up at night. Instead, he would get a piece of paper telling him to go elsewhere. In the ED I was to become the hospital's agent, the one who rousted the sick from the ED on the worst days—standing complicit on the best.

These plans weren't unique to our hospital; such changes were in motion across the country. And like other hospitals, our medical center, to blunt the damage, built a community partnership initiative to provide "the right care, in the right place, at the right time." While this work did link our clinical system with other health centers to provide primary care, the networks weren't big enough or strong enough or built quickly enough to match the pace of the hospital's cuts. The partnership's main effort became "educating" the community on where to get care, as though confusion on the part of the public was at the root of their health-care issues. There was no reconciling this process with a commitment to healing the community. I wasn't the only one who saw the immorality of these rushed and dangerous plans. My boss did too. And with the Patients of Distinction announcement, he stepped down, along with the head of internal medicine. We were without leadership as the storm of administrative changes buffeted us.

I was nauseous walking into the emergency faculty meeting convened in the wake of the resignations. In the two years of my first real job, two of my bosses had stepped down. Eight thousand ER patients would be pushed out to other sites. One hundred million dollars in budget cuts were rolled out without primary regard for patient safety. And now Patients of Distinction would take more services from ER patients. It became clear poor people, sick and without options, were being forced to balance the budget of the entire hospital. The CEO, his hastily appointed interim department chair, and a number of other administrators joined this meeting to discuss the internal upheaval and to lay out even further cuts. The current plans created an irreconcilable moral situation, and now we were going to go further? The whole thing was overwhelming. You were there, too. Did you know how it felt to watch people I looked up to ignore the droves of sick people who were being turned away? Did you know I wasn't sleeping anymore? Did you see the bags under my eyes?

I'd been in meetings with management before. Faculty engagement was a step in their operational planning process, but each time our input was considered superfluous. In the first meeting about reductions, a colleague of ours had pointed out how transferring asthma patients could deteriorate their condition by interrupting their ongoing treatment. The superiors called his feedback unproductive and told him he had failed to grasp the business imperative. Another colleague cited the research that showed increased mortality is a consequence of the long waits we were subjecting people to. Our administrators scorned her concerns as the musings of a wonky academic. Similarly, they'd rejected our moral and ethical questions with breezy rationalizations like "You have to break eggs to make an omelet," even though those "eggs" were people's bodies and lives. I knew that this faculty meeting would be no different. I expected what was going to happen next would be dictated in advance, not open to input.

The meeting began with the false cordiality of a divorce proceeding. A perfunctory welcome was followed by introductions to the CEO, the COO, and sundry managers. The executives wore blue and gray suits. The rest of us had on white coats, with tight jaws, furrowed brows, and pounding hearts. Flop sweat dampened my brow as I sat against the wall in the back. The central table was reserved for bureaucrats and senior faculty members—that's where you and your equals assembled. With no social banter and no side conversation, a tense silence ushered us quickly into business. Leadership boasted that they had no experience in the ED and scant exposure to the community that we serve but could do their work anyway using key principles. As expected, a "realignment of resources" was introduced. We'd be forced to transfer even more poor patients who called the surrounding neighborhood their home. Meanwhile, the Patients of Distinction would not only avoid transfer, but they would be treated in a special section of the ER reserved for their care.

The CEO planned to reorganize the Emergency Department with ten beds walled off and allocated to Patients of Distinction. Eight beds that had been used as a fast track for ankle sprains, coughs, and other minor complaints would be closed. Patients of Distinction made up not quite a fifth of the forty-seven thousand Emergency Department visits a year, and now they would take up almost half of the available space and resources. The crowding for the remaining 80 percent of patients would grow sharply, and so would their suffering. I was stunned. You raised your hand to lead us through this morass— at times gently supportive of the CEO's plans and in other moments mildly against them. I still wonder how you felt then. Were you truly conflicted? Did you feel you had no choice? Did you know this moment mattered?

As the meeting went on, I fidgeted, and my heart pounded. This was even worse than I could have imagined, but I couldn't find any words. Should I confront them? Ask a smart question? Ask a dumb one? I just remained mute and let my belly churn. I knew that separating patients into separate pods to deliver care was not unusual in emergency medicine. But doing so based on their ability to pay was unheard of. One of the senior faculty questioned whether this was legal, another asked whether we could see the plan on paper, a third wondered about patient safety in the already overcrowded ED. Each of these questions was batted down with business lingo. I imagined patients vanishing as fast as our questions, driven off by catch-phrases. "We will shrink to distinction" dispatched the seventy-nine-year-old woman delirious with fever to a hospital many miles away from her family. "Restricting resources will improve flow" and *poof* went the working man with a broken arm to search on his own for an orthopod who would accept him. "Culture trumps planning" relegated the young woman hearing voices to a state facility. "Value, efficiency, opportunity," and I could see a friend's grandfather die in the waiting room, just steps away from the care he sought. Money became concrete, people abstract.

When I got home, I realized how much the plan was going to racially segregate the ED. In this pre-Obamacare period, one in five Black people was uninsured, in comparison to one in eight white people. In the segregated context of Chicago's South Side these disproportions were amplified. While there were Black people with private insurance, almost all of our uninsured and publicly insured population was Black. Building a wall between the insured Patients of Distinction and the South Side's uninsured patients and patients with Medicare and Medicaid would effectively create one ER for white patients and another for Black people. The ED for Black patients would be challenged to serve many more patients in a much smaller space. Overcrowded and under-resourced, the ED would become a site where people would wait an intolerably long time for care. If friends, childhood teachers, or my parents arrived with a medical emergency, they would end up on the wrong side of that wall.

I'd come to the university to care for the community that raised me. Now, instead I was enrolled in a plan to flout *Brown v. Board of Education* in order to funnel precious health-care resources to Patients of Distinction. I was to be the Black cop restraining his neighbor, the Black prosecutor convicting his brother, the Black lender denying his sister's mortgage. A leak alerted the *Chicago Tribune* and *The New York Times* to the policies, and the American College of Emergency Physicians called these practices "dangerous," the same strategies that gave rise to the anti-dumping EMTALA laws. Did you know that I was resolved? I decided the day they segregated the ED would be the last day I showed up for a shift.

My coping practices in this period involved scotch, my couch, and angry texts with my peer group of young faculty members. Now months into the cost cutting, we'd stew and point out how obviously wrong their strategies were, how racist, how dangerous, and debate what we ought to do. Going along with the administration meant aligning with a great evil, and quitting meant defaulting on my educational debt. Hyperbolically, I referenced photos of SS guards picnicking with their families. This was all a reminder that the capacity to perpetuate evil doesn't mean people grow horns and hooves. Regular, normal people abide evil while loving their children and sharing laughs with friends. And here were doctors and leaders I knew well— including you—going along with a plan to discriminate and hurt people.

The meeting that proposed ED segregation crystallized the tension of those months. I prepared a letter to foreshadow what I assumed would be my inevitable resignation. I described the immorality of segregation in health care and how these ostensibly race-neutral reorganization plans would lead to such an outcome. The letter outlined how ethics (and the law) dictate that patient needs *alone* should organize emergency resources. Reviewing that email now, eleven years later, brings back those jittery fingers and the dry mouth. The note, full of typos, features a passive academic tone, but it is unambiguous. I sent that email to you and the other doctors who led when our bosses resigned. I needed you all to know: proceeding with this plan would mean "separate and unequal."

That email was forwarded around. Within a day the CEO called me on my cell phone to ask about it. He pushed me to consider that the intention of his plans was not to racially segregate and noted that the plans were entirely mute about race. I countered that whether it was intended or not, racial segregation would be the outcome. I couldn't ignore that, and neither should he. Before we ended the call, I offered a counterproposal to reorganize the ED with a basis in illness severity, not insurance status. That plan gained steam over the next few weeks through email and hallway conversations. Soon, fearful and depressed colleagues became emboldened to speak in favor of this new approach. My resignation became less inevitable with every passing day.

The next few weeks were consumed by working, but not on the research I was admonished to continue. Instead, I was partnering with quiet allies in the administration and organizing the hospital's young physicians. The immorality of a segregated ED offering wealthy and white patients quality care at the expense of services for poor and Black people fueled me through sleepless nights and anxiety about retaliation. No longer did I worry about my debt or mortgage. There could be no compromise that segregated or otherwise extracted resources from the poor. Not here. Not in an emergency room in the heart of the South Side. My mission was clear.

As you likely recall, ultimately the administration flinched. Plans to segregate the ED to benefit Patients of Distinction were replaced with a design to structure the space by illness severity. The administration would follow through on its pledge to reorganize care, but there would be no wall to separate patients and no separate ED for Patients of

Distinction. If implemented faithfully, this new plan to focus resources on patients based on the severity of their conditions could streamline care and incorporate community resources to extend its features.

By the time the smoke cleared a year later, we had lost a department head and four section heads. All of the emergency medicine faculty under thirty-five departed to restart their careers elsewhere. The CEO, COO, and CFO of the Medical Center disappeared as well. That punitive segregation plan took its toll on all of us. You were there— you must have known I couldn't stay. After four different bosses in three years, I couldn't grow there. And when people I respected showed me that they would accept segregation if it led to profit, I could no longer see myself as part of that community. I couldn't study inequity when processes were in motion to drive injustice. My hope for an academic career was snuffed out by the fight. I looked for my exit.

I write you years later to let you know that I am thankful for that time. I was forced to stare at the truth stripped of artifice and social grace. I saw firsthand how our institution is like so many American institutions: it was willing to destroy bodies as inputs to its profit function. I witnessed how our good people, like so many good Americans, acted as bystanders in the face of a monstrosity. I saw how decades of segregation and a biased distribution of health resources left the South Side sick, uninsured, and undesirable. How "color-blind" financial decisions transferred services from poor people to well-off people, taking from Black people and giving to white people, exploiting the racial sorting performed by society. I observed how health inequity is not simply the product of benign neglect waiting to be fixed but an active and intentional scheme to take from one community and give to another. I witnessed arguments that tried to elevate the importance of morality and science rendered impotent in the face of a financial imperative. The "right thing" was irrelevant. Only power mattered.

Do you remember those times, Richard? Do you remember where you stood in those moments of truth? When standing in the middle facilitated the evil of institutional segregation? Do you remember your decision to equivocate when so much was on the line? I do. It took time, but I have forgiven you and the rest in leadership as I know none of us are solely our biggest mistake or greatest triumph—all of us are complicated and flawed. I also came to recognize that the forces that wrought that period were bigger than you or me and bigger than this institution—they are the powers that define this country. That insight allowed me to return in order to resume service to my community. Now, about a decade later, I continue to treat patients here, and we remain in each other's lives. But I want you to know that those events changed me, changed you, and changed the hospital, even if only temporarily. I remember, and I'll never forget.

Onward,

tlf

12

SEPTEMBER 2020

IN THE SPRING COVID surge, the entire ambulance bay was enclosed and converted to a massive negative-pressure space for patients. Designed to park four massive Chicago Fire Department ambulances with enough space to unload their full stretchers, now it holds eight patient treatment coves, four on either side of a hallway. Separated by temporary six-foot-high walls, each cove has a gurney alone: no chair, no sink, nothing else. Makeshift alcohol hand-wash stations keep us clean, and portable monitors can be moved into the inlets to transmit patients' vital signs to screens in the main area of the Emergency Department. Within this massive garage, temporary yellow HVAC tubes snake across the twenty-foot-high ceiling. Air conditioning roaring through those pipes kept the space cool during the summer, and now they strain to keep this uninsulated area warm. While some hospitals erected tents to manage COVID, this invention was part of our resourceful response, and now we use it to keep up with rebounding patient volume.

Today I'm responsible for the patients in this makeshift area. To get there from the main emergency room I have two options. The first way is through the double doors opposite the nurse desk. Wide enough for two teams with stretchers to pass as one enters and one exits, this access is used mostly by paramedics who park their ambulance on the curb, unload their patient outside, then cut through the transformed ambulance bay on their way in. The second entrance is at the opposite end of the bay, through the decontamination chamber. With an enormous showerhead and massive drain that stand ready to douse patients and first responders who have been exposed to gasses or chemicals, it is sealed by locked doors on both the ambulance-bay side and the ER side. While cutting through the decon chamber is the fastest path from the doctor's workstations into the ambulance bay, I can't use it because today it holds a body.

After a long resuscitation attempt, the corpse of a patient who died on their way to the hospital was moved from a treatment room to the decontamination space until the morgue could pick it up. Normally we leave cadavers in the room where we tried to revive them so that families can see them and grieve, but COVID means no visitors. For every family the loss of a loved one is momentous, and we're still figuring out how to mark those events with the respect and gravity they deserve. But deaths in the ER happen almost daily, and we need every possible space to care for the sick patients in our full waiting room. For the next few hours, to avoid disturbing the dead, I'll enter the makeshift treatment area by using the double doors used by the paramedics.

After cleaning my workstation and signing onto the medical record, I go meet my first patient. Wearing clean blue scrubs from the machine and hidden behind a yellow surgical mask, goggles, and purple head cover, I'm in my hospital disguise. Between these anonymizing coverings and the long stretches alone, sometimes I feel invisible, but the greetings of familiar colleagues—"Fish!" "S'up, Dr. Fisher!"—remind me that I'm still right here. After a stroll from the work area past Rooms 41 through 45, I swipe my badge on the wall pad to open the double doors to the ambulance bay. Once I'm inside the cavernous area a patient waves and calls out, "Doc!" My cover is blown.

Today every space in the entire ER is filled with folks, living and dead. I glance over to make sure the patient—a man in a hat and mask who is holding a crutch—is not bleeding or presenting an obvious emergency. After a nod, I turn left and keep walking to the treatment coves. I know he's been waiting too long—they all have—but I can't help that right now. I look down to my feet to avoid further eye contact as I finish my stroll. My gray hospital sneakers have been in rotation since March and are now beat down. I feel like I'm walking barefoot across these concrete floors designed for trucks.

The patients I'm looking for are in Coves 3 and 6, which are right across from one another. The first is a COVID survivor. Ms. Favors is a generously proportioned sixty-nine-year-old woman in a hospital gown, pink camouflage mask, and pink head wrap. She was intubated in May and went home in July after a stint in rehab. In a new development, her legs are so swollen that she's having trouble getting around, so she came in to find out if anything could be done for her. I pull over a rolling stool and sit down next to her. I have to get close enough to her to hear what she says but stay far enough away to stay safe. I'm curious about her COVID hospitalization, but she can't tell me much about it—she doesn't remember. "They say my grand-daughter found me passed out in the bathroom partially dressed," she says. "She called 911, and they brought me here. I was on a ventilator, but I don't know anything about that. First thing I remember is being in a hospital bed until they transferred me to rehab." She told me it happened in April, but when I re-viewed her chart it said May. The neurologists think Ms. Favors's amnesia and cognitive difficulty come from COVID encephali-tis. Her course was so rocky it could have been any number of things. She's lucky to be alive.

In the bay next to us, a young woman with a broken arm is on the phone complaining loudly about her wait. Voices rever-berating in the open space and the air blowing from the exposed heating vents force me to focus harder to hear Ms. Favors. She has never had swelling like this before, and she ran out of her medications last week. "I got five grandkids to keep up with, I just couldn't get to the pharmacy. Then my legs swole up, and I could barely take care these kids."

"Ma'am, I think this swelling is from heart failure. The best next step would be to admit you here to get this fluid off and figure out why your heart is straining."

"Honey, there's no way. I have to take care of my grand-babies!" she yells to me over the noisy HVAC and the chatter bouncing off the concrete all around us, her eyes and hands ani-mated.

"Can you do what you did when you were in the hospital for those months?" I ask.

"Nope! Their mama was with us then."

"Where is she now?"

"Tennessee. I sent her away."

"Why?" I know it's none of my business, but I can't restrain my curiosity.

"Bless her heart. That's all I can say." She raises her eyebrows at me meaningfully to signal that our conversation is over.

Ms. Favors is one of the thousands of South Siders who were struck by COVID. But she was fortunate—she survived. By May, when Ms. Favors was hospitalized, Black people in Chicago, who are 29 percent of the population, made up 72 percent of the deaths. The situation was most acute for people who relied on others to protect them. Nursing home residents and workers made up a third of those who fell ill and a fifth of those who died. In one South Side facility, a predominantly Black nursing home with 240 beds, 121 residents fell ill and 24 died. Many of those patients came to my ED. The Cook County Jail, one of the nation's largest, also had an astronomical infection rate. Without PPE, unable to be tested, and crowded into holding areas, the incarcerated and the incarcerators were infected. South Side Black folks got sick in jail, and as they came home, they infected their families and neighbors.

Black Chicagoans on the South Side were exposed by a general public health strategy that failed to take responsibility for its citizenry and couldn't counter the falsehoods spread on social media. About four out of ten Black adults said they knew someone who had died from the coronavirus, almost double the rate for white people. Now, several months into the pandemic, we're seeing more survivors with lingering issues. While Ms. Favors is back in the world and back in the life of her family, COVID has robbed her of her memory and splintered her family. It's possible COVID caused this bout with heart failure. We're going to try to fix this and send her back to her people.

I walk across the way to Cove 6 and my next patient, a forty-one-year-old gentleman with pus leaking from the side of his abdomen. In a hospital gown, he wears a black mask that doesn't hide his salt-and-pepper beard or his nervous eyes. There's no chair to rest in, so I lean against the gurney he's lying on by putting my knee on the bed. He tells me he was shot in the belly two years ago and now, from time to time, pus leaks from one of his wounds.

"Can I see that wound, Mr. Jones?"

"Yes, sir! Happy to show you."

He's cheerful and using formal language, a sure sign he's seen too many doctors.

"When I was shot it ripped my colon. Ever since then, I get these abscesses. Usually, a surgeon comes and drains it."

We don't have the benefit of complete privacy, given the temporary walls that only close on three sides, but I slide a screen over to help. He spreads open his hospital gown and lifts his black T-shirt to reveal a belly that looks like a garden plot. Brown like the soil, with rows formed by the deep scars where surgeons opened him, left colostomies, and closed him up again. In one of those ruts is an umbilicated wound that spills pus onto a piece of gauze. I can smell the stench through my mask. "Are you in any pain?" I ask.

"No, sir. It hurt yesterday, but now it feels better."

Mr. Jones is a middle-aged survivor of a different plague attacking the South Side. At first COVID—and the quarantine and the rapid decline in economic activity—halted violence: a national study showed that homicide rates fell in thirty-nine of sixty-four major cities during April. But the numbers began creeping up in May. And then Chicago exploded. A *New York Times* article I saw captured the mood: "'The Windy City is becoming the Bloody City,' said the Rev. Michael L. Pfleger of Saint Sabina Church, calling it the worst period in the forty-five years he has worked on social issues. 'I have never seen the despair, hopelessness and anger all mixed together at the level it is right now.'"

The kind of violence that ripped open Mr. Jones's belly is isolated to just a few swaths of the city and country. Nationally, we know that more than a quarter of gun homicides take place in about 1,200 neighborhoods that house just 1.5 percent of the population. In Chicago these killings are concentrated in the zip codes around my hospital and on the West Side. Tensions caused by the lockdown's economic toll peaked at the same time informal mediators like clergy and elders were shut in or killed by COVID. Schools, community centers, churches, and gyms were all shuttered, eliminating diversions that help keep a lid on violence. Further, conflict de-escalation groups were undermined by the physical distancing required to avoid COVID. Daily shootings and their retaliations headlined the local news, then became so mundane that the carnage was reduced to statistics.

For decades folks in South Side neighborhoods have done all they could to end the killing. The solutions have ranged from block clubs that organize neighborhood watches and provide social outlets for teens to violence interventions that deescalate conflict in the moment to demands for a South Side trauma center. Today I work in the trauma center that was sought for decades by people in the community, and we are saving lives, like that of Mr. Jones. But by the time people come to me full of holes, we've already lost. These folks, like Mr. Jones, won't ever be the same, physically or mentally. And even our best trauma care doesn't reduce the number who come to us riddled with bullets.

I can get these two patients home today and back to their everyday lives. But those lives will never return to the way they were before their bodily tragedies. So many months into this pandemic and it's clear that on top of all the everyday health problems, gun violence and COVID are stealing the lives of Black folks, ruining families, and destabilizing communities. While these scourges burn all across the country, people on the South Side—Black people, poor people—fell into the pyre while those on the North Side—wealthy people, white people—were barely singed. Each of my COVID patients has their own specific story about how they caught the virus. Every one of my gun-wounded patients has a private, individual narrative for how they got shot. But they are part of a larger pattern. I'll get Mr. Jones a CT for his abdomen and talk to the surgeons if there's a deeper infection, but I've got nothing today for these grinding spirals of inequality.

On my way out of the ambulance bay and back to the work area, I pass a woman vomiting over the garbage. A nurse goes to her with an emesis bag, and I help her to a chair. She's forty-eight and tells us that she's always nauseous after dialysis. Ever since her dialysis session last night she's been vomiting, she hasn't been able to sleep, and now she's feeling weak. She lets us know that she comes in every couple of months like this, and each time we do tests, and if they're okay, she goes home. Her black puffy jacket seems like it's far too warm for the early fall day. We help her out of it, and her nurse starts searching her arm for a vein where she can insert an IV. We may as well start treating her right there in the stopgap waiting area. I head back to my desk, document care for the two patients I met and then, for the vomiting woman, I order medicine for her nausea and labs to ensure her electrolytes are okay.

Now three hours into the shift, the body has been removed from the decontamination chamber. While most of the Emergency Department is socked in with admitted patients who wait for an inpatient bed, the waiting room's population is growing. The ambulance bay is the only area where we can see patients, and I traipse back and forth through the free decon room to get there. After hearing from the residents and discussing options, I interview and examine two or three people at a time. I never carry my stethoscope—between the din of the open room and the risk of being too close to COVID patients, it's just not worth trying to listen to hearts and lungs. Instead, I rely on blood tests and radiology to outline what's going on.

After I hear from a senior resident, I go to Cove 2 to meet a confused patient. There I find a cachectic sixty-year-old woman whose wan and bony face is shielded behind a white mask. Her kind eyes, sunken by weight loss, are expressive, and her skeletal hands fumble with her gown. "Hi ma'am, you doing okay?" While holding eye contact, she moves her head and hands but mostly just stammers incoherently, "Uh, well, you know." So I slow down and ask yes-no questions.

"Are you in pain?"

"No."

"Do you know where you are?"

"Yes."

"Is it normal for you to have trouble with words?"

"Yes. Ever since the. . . ." I know she means the tumor they found in her brain—I read about it in her chart, and her resident shared the details. She survived breast cancer earlier in her life, but now it has recurred and has spread to her brain and her lung. I stop asking questions and review the portable monitor. Her vital signs are stable. Her right chest wall is a hard, lumpy, purple mass, and on the left her ribs are showing. I glance back up at her face: drawn and pale, ringed by thin gray hair. I notice two fentanyl patches on her left arm and remove them. Her confusion could be worsened by too much of that narcotic. She winces as I probe her belly and touch her legs—her whole body is sensitive and in pain. I know she's not long for us. I'll update the resident with my findings, and we'll search for the trigger of her confusion with CTs of her head and belly and also hunt for infections.

As I leave her bedside, I am struck silent by the gravity of her illness. In the ER we see only those being beaten by cancer's campaign or people experiencing treatment side effects. Patients who have uneventful cancer therapy and reach remission never come to the ER. Even though I recognize the skewed sample that I serve, cancer still terrifies me with its nausea, recurrences, and pain. Control in life is said to be illusory—cancer brings that maxim into relief. She's no longer the person she was, now closer to death than life. I'm rescued from these thoughts by the sight of an old friend.

Craig is a stocky, clean-shaven Black man who rides Ambulance 55—the notorious "double nickel." Craig was a tech in the ER when I was a resident, and we've been cool ever since. He's got a fifty-eight-year-old gentleman, Mr. Flood, on his stretcher, brought in because of a laceration on his leg.

"Bruh, wait till you see it, this ain't no normal laceration."

"Uh-oh, what are we talking about here?"

"Oh, I won't spoil it, but I'm bringing you some serious work."

We walk together to Room 38 and I help them transfer the patient to the gurney from the ambulance stretcher. A nurse and resident join me. The patient has on a blue mask, baggy jeans, Timberlands, and a white tank top. The jeans aren't stained by blood, and there's no sign of trauma. I say, "Okay, let's see this injury." Mr. Flood pulls up his right pants leg, gingerly unwraps the gauze that was applied on the way to the hospital, and displays a six-inch wound. Midway between the knee and ankle of his right leg the gash is ragged, dry, and so deep you can see the muscles and tendons moving as he tries to adjust his semi-flaccid ankle. I look at the residents and nurses, who are transfixed by the wound. "See, I told you," notes Craig on his way out of the room.

Mr. Flood is a little bit disheveled and makes the kind of furtive eye contact that leaves people uncomfortable but unable to say why. When the resident asks what happened, he says, "Somebody tried to cut my leg off with a knife."

"What the hell?" remarks his nurse to nobody in particular. He continues that he went to his girlfriend's house and the custodian—or was it her other boyfriend, or maybe it was the security guard, or perhaps her roommate—pinned him down and tried to cut his leg off with a knife. With each follow-up question the assailant changes, but he is clear that a man tried to sever his leg. He lets us know he got out of there, though he can't say just how, went home, and sort of waited. Although it happened three days ago, today was the first day he felt well enough to come to the hospital, so he called 911.

Further questions are evaded with a stutter and side-eye. The story didn't add up. Was it a fight? Did he call the police? Why didn't he come to the hospital when it happened? Does it hurt? There are no satisfying or realistic answers to any of these questions. How does one lie around for days with a partially amputated leg after being in a fight for his life? And yet here he is. Back at the workstation, his resident calls the orthopedic surgery team whose job will be to repair his leg and ensure he doesn't get an infection. At the end of the call, she reports that they are confused by the weird story and are going to come down to see it for themselves.

I have no way to process the intimate and ferocious violence that creates that injury. The lives involved and the stories that led to this surreal brutality are hard for me to fully conjure, and the effort makes my head spin. I need a break. I rub alcohol wash on my hands and amble over to the telemetry radio room for a cup of coffee. As my paper cup fills from the carafe on the counter outside the room, I peek inside to say hello to the telemetry nurse. She looks up from her smartphone to say "What's up," then returns her gaze to the screen. Before COVID there were groups in there chatting all day—this was the office "watercooler." Now alone, the radio nurses are glued to their phones between calls. What looks like lack of interest is actually decompression between unfiltered human experiences. In a world of sleek social media and fake news, seeing the unadulterated bodies of our savaged patients feels like looking in a funhouse mirror. While real, they appear distorted, and they outnumber us, forcing us to sometimes wonder whether it is we who are misshapen. I watch the nurse slowly drag her finger around her phone's screen, and I can't fault her. It's safer to have a social media algorithm and purified photos focus our eyes on things anodyne and pleasant.

Muddy, burnt coffee at the end of the pot is all that's left. It's not tasty, but caffeine is caffeine. I'll have good coffee at home— right now I just need a jolt. On days like this, we're so full that only the sickest patients make it to a room. It takes hours to get to the young people with headaches or the women who are having abnormal bleeding. When I return to the workstation the residents inform me of three more people in the ambulance bay that are waiting to be seen. Two have cancer, and one has sickle cell anemia. The folks who are prioritized in this overburdened system are really complicated. I miss the days of peak COVID, when I was less busy, but where were these patients then? It's unlikely that they were miraculously cured when COVID shut down the city. I wonder, did they just stay home and die in March and April?

I head to the ambulance bay to meet each of the three new patients in their coves. The first is an eighty-year-old woman. She is short of breath and has lung cancer, or at least "that's what they tell me." She lets me know she's skeptical of her diagnosis when I ask about it.

"Do you think that's wrong?" I ask.

"Well, I just don't know. Fourteen years ago, they found a lump in my lung. It wasn't bothering me, so I left it alone. I got a new doctor last year, and they put a camera in my chest to see why I was having trouble breathing. Again they saw it and said it was cancer. But cancer patients have pain and are sick. Now I have been losing weight, but I'm not sick. I just have trouble breathing sometimes like everyone else. I don't know what's wrong. I feel it's my body, and I'd know if I had cancer. But my family trusts them, so here I am."

"I'm with you. I understand. What do you think it is if it's not that?"

Tears well up. One by one they spill over and stream down each side of her face, but through it all her voice remains even. "The chemotherapy is worse than the disease. If it might not be cancer, why should I have therapy?"

"I see that too. I know people suffer with cancer treatment. But it does give some people more time and others get cures."

"That's what my kids say. So I keep coming to the doctors. They say these docs are good. But when it's time to get into details, they go outside my room and talk with each other for twenty minutes and only talk to me for five. I know they're keeping things from me."

"Wow, I never thought of it like that," I say. "I spend extra time talking to the residents to teach them, but I can see how it looks."

"Doc, you're taking your time with me. They don't do that. They just tell me what to do." Thin as a rail under her hospital gown, in a dark wig and with nails painted purple, she seems willing. After all, she keeps coming back, even if only out of love of her kids. But mistrust and fear are preventing her from embracing what's going on. "My sister died here. I don't want to die here too." She's uncertain about the strange symptoms and distant doctors. Unsure what she should anchor to, she connects to what she knows. That means she's soldiering on.

I've spent twenty minutes perched on the corner of her bed

in an alcove surrounded by temporary walls. My hope is that she'll trust me enough to grapple with the cancer. But I can only start that process and gamble that her oncologist picks up the thread from here. In the ED there are always more patients to see, and if I don't keep moving, I'll never get to the queue. So I ask her if we can do tests to make sure she doesn't have fluid in her chest or a clot in her lungs. She agrees. When I offer an elbow bump on my way out, she grabs my hand and holds it. I don't say anything, I just nod. She nods back.

In the next cove is a fifty-three-year-old woman with HIV and lung cancer that is metastatic to her liver. I remain standing this time because my hip is sore from the weird position I had to hold on the bed of the previous patient. "Hey now, I'm Dr. Fisher, I heard from your resident that your stomach hurts. Is that right?"

"Yeah, Doc. It hurts so bad that I can't eat," she says. She lets me know that for two weeks she's had terrible belly pain and trouble eating. Every time she eats, she gets nausea and so she stopped and only drinks fluids. She has been losing weight, maybe fifteen pounds by now.

I notice that under her hospital gown she has weathered brown skin that's wrinkled and sagging from her body. The corners of her eyes crinkle when she talks, and her weary eyes connect with mine through our conversation. After a couple minutes my hip stops hurting, so I sit down on the bed by her feet. I wonder about the HIV and what she takes for it. She said she caught HIV years ago when she was addicted to heroin. Now she's on methadone, and medications have rendered her HIV undetectable. When I ask about her stomach and how long she's been sick, she lets me know she was diagnosed a while ago with lung cancer that had spread to her liver. Her stomach has been racked with cancer pain on and off for a year now. She tears up when she talks about it. The pain pursues her into her sleep, waking her at odd hours, and it keeps her from eating or finding peace. Yesterday she visited a different hospital, and they brushed her off. "They gave me Tylenol but did not do a CT scan. How do you know I'm okay if you didn't even look? They treated me like trash!"

"Damn. I'm so sorry you experienced that. Did you leave feeling any better?"

"What do you think? I just kept vomiting, and they still ran me up out of there. Y'all are my doctors, so I came here today." She's right. We've been treating her cancer for a few months now, and it looks like she's almost due for her next therapy. "When will they give me treatment?" she asks. "I hope today. I need something. I can't even eat."

Her resident is an intern who is from the West Coast. Earnest and hardworking, she's worried that narcotic pain medications could complicate the patient's recovery from opioid abuse. But given the advanced cancer and intense pain, she may not have long. Fentanyl is a good choice, but it will only address the suffering that comes from pain. I don't have anything for the disrespect she's experienced, the despair that may accompany her end, or the loneliness that results from addiction driving family from her life. Still, during our conversation, her tears dry, we laugh, and I touch her shin. As I prepare to leave, I ask her if there is anything else I need to know. She grabs a fistful of my scrub pants in her gaunt hand, furrows her brow, and says, "Just take care of me. . . ."

Finally, in the cove across the hall is a woman with sickle cell anemia who is having her usual pain crisis. The resident managing her care has already ordered labs to be drawn and shared her story with me. When I enter the cove, I realize I've seen her multiple times over the years. She's in her late twenties and is wearing gold wire-frame glasses, a brown satin bonnet, and leopard-print pajamas. She generally gets pain in her limbs and sometimes wants to stay for IV pain medications, but not today. Today, she cannot wait to get back home, because she does not want to catch the monster. "Please just give me a shot so I can go home."

"Are you sure? We ordered labs and an IV to check you out thoroughly."

"No way. I do *not* want to be here. I just ran out of my medications at home."

While we are seeing patients sick with all kinds of diseases, there are still a lot of people infected with the virus. It's smart to stay away if she can. "Absolutely. I got you."

With that I get up, wash my hands, and head back through the decon room to the workstation. So far, my patients are gasping for breath, are consumed by cancer, or have been ripped open by bullets. While each began with an acute event, now they all have chronic problems that I cannot cure. They all face a steady decline to the end, but that end will not be today. Death defines 2020. For more than six hundred thousand people, COVID's quarantine means that they share their final sputtering breaths with health-care workers and no one else. Then the dying victims of a national—no, global—tragedy are buried without fanfare or presidential salute at Dover. Some people, including politicians, even deny that those deaths happened. Even as fatalities rise on the South Side, the city doesn't stop to take notice. There are too many for their names to be listed in the paper. Instead their bodies become fodder for debate and contribute to upward-pointing graphs. Few witness the consequences of these public health failures. But here in the ED we see it all, whether the victims die in our arms or just beyond the screens we hold up to our faces to escape for just a moment.

When I finally get back to my home in the West Loop, after I've deposited my scrubs in the laundry and washed off the hospital grime, I walk to the grocery store to replenish my fridge. It's tranquil. Fully stocked, ripe bananas and yogurt on sale. Bearded hipsters in Off-White sneakers buy fresh salmon. Women in $150 yoga pants load up on snacks. If not for masks and a proliferation of plexiglass screens it would seem that everything is normal. But the South Side is not at all normal. It's a jumble of sickness, violence, and COVID. Even as I'm largely protected in my neighborhood, my patients are suffocated by the virus and shot full of holes. Their dead bodies wait to be taken to the morgue while I work, wrapped in plastic and breathing through a filter, to prevent that outcome for others who are febrile and bleeding. Segregation means that on the North Side of town folks can maintain the illusion that things aren't that bad so long as the stock market stays afloat. Straddling these two worlds makes me insane. Is this grocery store real, or is what I've experienced and seen in the hospital real? Because they cannot both be real.

Or can they?

13

Dear Ms. Favors,

You came to me short of breath, and you were still laboring when you departed to take care of your grandkids. Your heart failure came after a long and rocky COVID course. We didn't offer you much help for your heart failure or your family situation. You looked for answers, but what we gave you created more questions. While we treated you the best we could, it must all look ridiculous to you, health care that doesn't really care, a system designed by people in nice offices who, try as they might, fail to make it better. I know this because I've been in offices like that. I was an executive and worked alongside smart, kindhearted people trying to make your path easier. I want to tell you why I failed.

I rose every morning hours before my alarm. While it was still dark outside, I'd put on running shoes and hit the streets. In those quiet mornings, amber streetlights flickered off, and the streets were peaceful except for delivery trucks, my pounding feet and heavy breaths. As the miles reeled past, I'd tell myself that expanding health insurance to the most vulnerable was happening for the first time in fifty years and I was fortunate to contribute. And while stretching, I'd reassure myself that I'd offer valuable experience and skills once I overcame the challenges involved in learning a new culture. In a couple hours I'd be showered, suited, and lost in my corner office. After a hospital-wide conflict over segregating the ER, I abandoned academia and left a familiar community. Adjusting to this corporate environment took months, and my daily runs guided me through that disorientation. Then, every Friday, my weekly ER shift reminded me that patients like you were the only reason to forge into the wilderness of a new sector.

Anxiety burned away in those early-morning runs. After experiencing the fervor of health reform as a White House Fellow in the Obama administration, I joined an insurance company as it followed through on Affordable Care Act implementation. The ACA called for health insurance marketplaces where uninsured people could buy subsidized health insurance. In addition, much of the planned Medicaid expansion was going to be delivered through private enterprises. Here was my chance to resolve conflicts between the way we pay for health care and the services you need.

For the first year my task was to learn the company's people, culture, and language. It was as humbling as studying abroad, or my first exposures to the hospital wards. While I understood the ACA, I was naive to the intricacies of administering insurance. Benefit plans, networks, and claim adjudication were straightforward ideas on paper but required complex mechanisms to deliver. Company workers faithfully deployed instruments and processes refined over decades. Pivoting the enterprise toward the ACA's new rules would be onerous, but that disruption was a chance to reimagine everything. If it's true that we get what we pay for, then the ACA gave us a chance to question dangerous incentives like the ones that led my hospital to envision ER segregation. Instead, we could entice providers to serve patients justly and efficiently.

In my first few months the company's leaders led every meeting with new principles and stories of change to get the team inspired. One tale that lingers with me is an anecdote about the custodians at NASA who did not see their work as emptying wastebaskets—no, they were putting people into space! I always wondered whether that story was true. It didn't matter. True or not, memes inspired our work to "turn the battleship" and "learn the lessons of Kodak." Shared stories wove together our massive organization to prepare for change.

A mentor coached my transition into this new way of working. Her name was Karen. Her office was in the C-suite on the twentieth floor. Behind the locked doors, wide hallways were hung with original art, giving it all an air of tranquility. Plush carpeting hushed my steps to her office. She'd greet me at her door, offer a smile and a warm "Hello." Her shelves were an orchestrated mix of plants, photos, and knickknacks that reflected a corporate designer's style. Once the door was closed, formality disappeared—Karen had grown up on the South Side many years before me and was closer to your age than mine. Polished by decades of experience in the organization, she knew where all the dangers lay, and she'd share stories of Black leaders who had stumbled into traps along the way.

Getting crossways with informal leaders was a common obstacle. One Black exec moved too fast, another didn't have senior support, the next failed to build momentum. A few fought unwinnable battles, became frustrated, and gave up. She let me know change is usually consumed by the inertia of the organization, which is already optimized to do exactly what it is currently doing. But ACA implementation presented an opening to try new things—if there was ever a time

to make things better for patients like you, it was now. She encour-
aged me to take my time, learn the history of the organization, and get
to know the leaders. Before we adjourned our meetings, she'd draft
an introductory email to a leader she thought was interesting and encourage the two of us to grab lunch.

I don't remember most of those lunches. I often ordered salmon
Caesar salads and Diet Cokes. There were handshakes and kind
greetings. Maybe we'd discuss how we ended up at the company, the
Cubs versus the White Sox, or the weather. It was in those many
lunches where I practiced this new language and culture. Over count-
less coffees with colleagues I'd blow on my cup until it was cool
enough to sip, ask about their family, and listen. Over time I gathered
a cadre of allies, a few enemies, and a couple people I still speak to
almost every day. Persuasion in this culture was distinct from my experiences in our community, government, or academia. Stories mattered as much as data, neutral dispassion was superior to appearing
to care too much, profit and efficiency infused all topics, but relationships prevailed above all.

I slowly gained aptitude, getting humbled along the way just the
way I was in my first year of residency. What were my competitors
doing? What do organizational leaders support? Could I improve the
strength of our networks? What anecdotes should I be collecting and
retelling? Can I save money? What ideas can we promote to external
stakeholders? Jargon and questions that might be meaningless to
you were just as irrelevant to me before I adapted to this new community. It took me months to figure out how to build a case for systems that would acknowledge the challenges back home.

But there were costs to becoming proficient in these languages,
rules, and incentives. As I gained dexterity with executive culture, I

fumbled the words necessary to describe us—to describe the kinds of obstacles you're up against. Business argot couldn't convey the urgency of the defiant yells from the patients in the ED waiting room. Corporate settings dull the poetry of love and transcendence required to explain what's at stake when we're dealing with people's bodies and lives. I needed to share stories like yours; but without emotion, those truths lost their authority in a world of glass elevators, full bellies, and flush bank accounts. As with any endeavor that I worked on, it was working on me at the same time. I came to realize how easy it is to lose sight of the intimate and human purpose of health care when institutional language and processes obscure those heavy truths.

Even as I learned to direct teams and wield business tools, little changed for the people I served in the ER every Friday. Even now, years later, I could see that we—you as a patient, I as your physician— are just as trapped as my patients and I were when I began practicing twenty years ago. Maneuvering a health-care corporation to serve the most vulnerable would take a lifetime of work, and maybe three lifetimes. I'd have to climb my way into the tiny rooms where CEOs and board members initiate their plans. Along the way I was at risk of losing the ability to see what needed repair.

What if I could use these tools somewhere else? With my growing organizational skills, maybe I could make a durable impact with a smaller, more nimble enterprise, a startup. There I could set strategy without waiting decades. Maybe I could hire passionate people and lead the organization in a principled direction. Then, with the right people and the right culture, I might guide financial incentives to make health care safe and responsive to the most vulnerable. After four years I left the company and joined a fledgling managed-care organization as its first president. Focused on Chicago, I would serve my patients as both their doctor and their insurer. Here was the chance to hire from the community, support Black vendors, and drive systemic change.

It was a daunting task, but if we were successful we would transform care for thousands of people. First, we'd have to build an enterprise capable of managing health care. This meant constructing complex systems to send out insurance cards, complete health risk assessments, and pay medical claims—functions that must operate smoothly whether we had one member or one million members. Next, we would need to hire and train difficult-to-find and expensive care managers, nurses, and social workers in order to manage our members' illnesses. We would assemble a company out of thin air while being watched closely by state and federal regulators. Only then could we deliver incentive structures that would improve care in the way you seemed to intuitively understand was your right.

It wasn't long before ideals collided with money. Every month the state was supposed to send us an adjusted payment associated with each member. In this way, as our membership grew or became sicker, our reimbursement would grow to keep up. But that is not what happened. While we did get paid regularly, too often our promised income was delayed or incomplete. Unreliable cash flow forced us to decide which hires could wait and what parts of our foundation would be shortchanged. Many of the health-care providers who serve low-income members hang by a thread. We couldn't starve them. The technology and systems needed to meet regulatory requirements were expensive, and delaying or cutting corners there would leave us unable to function. Delaying payroll was out of the question. Wrestling with impossible financial and regulatory options meant hours of meetings, angry calls from vendors, and rapidly graying hair. Something had to give.

But we muddled forward. In our second year, now with tens of thousands of members and hundreds of employees, unpredictable cash flow contorted us into bizarre arrangements. We ignored our wealthiest creditors and skimped on employee benefits. Being incapable of building a sound institution and managing care at the same time felt like being a passenger in a car speeding toward a tree: I couldn't steer, couldn't stop, and couldn't get out. We had to court investors for more resources, slow our growth, or cut back on our obligations. I was happy to sacrifice growth and profitability for the opportunity to build the enterprise of my dreams. But the board and other leaders had different sentiments.

After many years, I was finally in the room where the most consequential decisions were made. But what if securing a just outcome required that the group unlearn decades of teaching, follow paths hidden by societal norms, and choose equity over self-interest? What if doing right by the least among us required the direction of something deeper than industry knowledge? In late-night phone calls and morning text conversations, we debated the path forward. Ultimately a decision was made: slash costs and shine up our balance sheet in order to pursue investors.

This required laying off employees, and not just any workers: we would fire our patient navigators. Navigators were the people who helped patients manage their thorny medical problems by tackling difficult social situations, getting them to their appointments, and filling their prescriptions. Our lowest-paid personnel, they were hired from the South and West Side communities we served. The majority were high school graduates; we trained them to find individuals, assess their health risk, and link them to care. They were critical to transforming our members from files on a screen to people in their community.

To me this decision felt like a moral failing, but for many on the board, the founders, and my senior team it was a simple business process—nothing to worry about. I was admonished that company presidents like me should not think too hard but simply execute. In their eyes, pushing the issue further undermined my own authority and leadership. I let it go. We prepared severance, résumé workshops, and mental health support, and finally chose a day for the announcement. I would present along with the head of HR. Where was my conviction from years earlier, to leave rather than participate in injustice? I was torn between my commitment to the organization and my conviction that we should protect the least among us. Unable to raise funds, improve our cash flow, meet our obligations, or buy the time necessary to find a moral solution, I was not getting enough sleep and feeling like a failure.

The auditorium filled soon after we arrived. I had stopped wearing ties when I left the corporation, so I wore a crisp white shirt and dark blue suit. Funeral wear. I followed my routine—the same breakfast, the same route to the auditorium—doing my best to replicate a regular day. But it wasn't regular at all. Folks who were called into the meeting had an inkling of what was coming. They'd seen the news about how hard things were for the state's managed-care plans, and they'd noted that this meeting was not for everyone in the organization. I cannot remember my script clearly, but I know I thanked them for their hard work and described how important they were. I told them we would hire them back if finances changed. Standing in front, I delivered my lines. My voice didn't crack. I didn't fidget. But I turned something off inside, and in a way that felt familiar. I had been trained to continue an ED shift, even after a patient dies.

After I said my piece, HR took over. They shared what would happen next, and I drifted toward the back of the room. To avoid eye contact I became acquainted with the brown flecks in the gray floor tiles. To my surprise, after we were done folks weren't angry or hurt. Many came forward to shake my hand. One man about ten years my junior, in jeans, a burgundy shirt, and sharp gray wool tie, told me, "It's not your fault, Doc. You gave us a shot. I really appreciate that." Maybe that was true, maybe not. Maybe we'd find an investor and could rehire these folks. Maybe this was the beginning of the end. Maybe I should have stepped down along with them.

Within a year we won an investor. Soon after that I was gone, and a few years later the entire organization disappeared. I gave nights, weekends, and all I had to construct an organization that committed to people. In the process, I learned there are no heroes. The same social and industry rules apply to every organization, and almost everyone is persuaded or crushed by that ethos. In the end I realized that I had become an agent of the schemes that I had vowed to combat—I was the one in a suit. It was I who stood in front of that auditorium and laid off every person there. I chose which corners to cut. While I had victories along the way, in the moment that mattered, I failed.

In the many years I worked in the business of health care, I faced only a few tests of my humanity and integrity. Most of the time, what was good for the institution aligned with what benefited the people we employed and served. This generated a virtuous cycle: the more our enterprises grew and profited, the more we could improve the lives of people in our community. Every day, we estimated when we couldn't measure, wrangled stray technology, and raced to meet deadlines, fueling a sequence of success. Collaborating day in and day out refined people and processes toward order and stability. But what about those critical instances when profitability and morality were opposed? What about decisions that determine who has easy access to emergency care in a downturn or who can afford lifesaving treatments? When organizations face challenges to their direction or viability, those same teams, tools, and practices can hurt people.

And so hardworking, kind, well-meaning people tirelessly maintain our broken status quo and find comfort in superficially neutral decisions that inflame injustice. In a moment where it mattered most, I couldn't drive a responsible organization to overcome the forces of a society that promotes profit over people.

Your health care is unresponsive to your needs because organizations fail to make moral decisions when it matters. These patterns are less common when there's enough for everyone, but as soon as there are financial challenges, your care becomes expendable. Like many before me, I have struggled to make the American health-care system more humane. After a decade, I am no longer naive. While most of what happens in the ER is beyond the control of both of us, the stakes are clear to us even as they become blurry from the vantage point of the boardroom. We're trapped here, yes, but the good news is that we are trapped together. Even behind masks, with limited time, we can see each other fully, bodily, and humanely, if we focus. Your challenges are my responsibility, and my rewards don't conflict with your health. Even if I cannot help you, I am trying.

Onward,

tlf

14

NOVEMBER 2020

"TOMMY, MOM IS IN pain." It's midmorning on Election Day. I'm lolling in bed, scrolling Twitter for voter-suppression stories. Lilla starts our morning FaceTime with a jolt rather than the usual check-in with my niece. Today they're at our parents' house, and this terse opening sits me up in bed.

"Damn. Can you put her on?"

"Yeah. Let me go find her."

I had planned to spend the day distracted from nonsense TV polls by reading, connecting with friends, and running outside. It is forecast to be a sunny 72 degrees—perfect for June, outrageous for late fall. It's November, and it hasn't been warm this late in the year since 2008, when Barack Obama was elected president of the United States. Twelve years ago, friends from all over the country filled with "Hope" convened in Chicago that balmy Election Day. We danced with strangers in streets secured by the Secret Service. I had similar optimism for this

Election Day until I heard of Mom's soreness. Mom never complains.

Lilla spent the night in Hyde Park and found her in the kitchen sitting in front of an untouched breakfast.

"Ma, what's wrong?" I ask, now up and out of bed. Her forced smile doesn't fool me.

"Oh, nothing. My side hurts a little, and I had trouble sleeping."

"A little?!" For her, "a little" could describe getting hit by a bus.

"Yeah, no big deal. Maybe it's another kidney stone. Some Tylenol will probably do it." While she wears a smile and holds her chin high, her eyes are dull, and she appears to have lost weight.

"Ma, do you want to go see about it? I'm worried."

"Yeah, maybe so."

My maternal great-grandmother lived past 103 despite having never been to a hospital, either for illness or for childbirth. With that tradition, my mother's willingness to see a doctor is telling.

"Okay. Where do you want to go? Your doctor's ER, or where I work?"

After a beat she says, "I'll go to yours."

"That sounds good. I'll let them know you're coming."

I have seen too many people languish for hours in our waiting room. After checking the schedule online, I text an on-shift colleague, Courtney, to let her know my mom is headed in. If nothing else, I need to be sure Mom isn't ignored or exposed to COVID while she waits. Courtney responds, "I will let the charge nurse know, and we'll get her in ASAP." I hope that they'll take good care of her and find something minor, so we can get back to normal. But I know better. Soon Dad texts me that Mom is showered and ready, he's grabbing his keys and bringing the car around.

By now it's just after noon, and I head out for a run. Usually I leave my phone at home so I can jog without interruption, but today I can't miss texts—so I run with the phone in my hand, ringer on. As I run west, the UPS Store is boarded up, Subway is secured with a metal grate, and a bunker of plywood guards the ground floor of the Ogilvie Transportation Center. The city rehearsed shuttering during the summer protests, and it has retreated like a turtle into its shell with the threat of election violence. When my phone finally vibrates, I stop running. It's Mom.

"Ok I'm here."

"Great!" I text in reply. I'm just beginning to breathe hard. I'm standing on a corner in front of a still-open 7-Eleven. I dash a note to Courtney. "She just hit the door."

"Bed 17 when it is clean. I just said hi to her. She is getting triaged now."

"Thank you!!"

This is all that I can hope for, an escort around the hurdles. Now I'm running on the sunny side of the street, past a handyman nailing plywood over the front door of a coffee shop. Soon I'm stopped again by my buzzing phone.

I read: "I'm in Room 17. The staff is very nice and hold you in high regard."

Feeling reassured, I "like" the message, pick up my pace, and head toward home with the sun in my face.

Panting and sweating, I turn the final corner for a sprint. I finish with my hands on my knees and my heart pounding. My legs feel warm and my calves twitchy. Running in the sun reminds me of being a teenager at track practice. If not for my laborious pace, it could be June 1994. Looping a mudcloth face mask over my ears to enter my building reorients me to 2020. During my climb up eight flights of stairs, the colleague who is caring for my mom texts me that she has permission to discuss the case and that my mother's vital signs are normal, and so far the labs are normal too. I dash off a reply thanking her and then text my mom to ask whether she's feeling okay.

"I'm doing ok."

"How is your pain?"

"A little better, I think."

"Have they given you anything?"

"Yes, I'll just let it work."

Why is my mom still hurting if everything is okay? Maybe it's a kidney stone, but what about an aortic aneurysm or pneumonia? I am out of breath and at my door, and doubt takes over.

"The pain is back."

My ears flame red when I read the message, and heat flushes my face. Even though more than an hour has elapsed, I'm still in workout clothes in my kitchen. My mother is still awaiting the result of her abdominal CT. I've passed time reading and talking to friends on a group chat called "Free the Land." It's time for shift change in the ED, a notoriously risky period where details sometimes get dropped.

"Ok ma, did you ask for pain medication?"

"I did a while ago, but I haven't gotten anymore."

I don't want my mom to suffer, but neither do I want to direct her care. I'm not her doctor—I'm her son.

"Ok, give them another 15 minutes and let me know."

Things had proceeded smoothly, but now she's slid from VIP care to being just another Black lady in pain. Fifteen minutes elapse, and with no signs of relief, I have to jump in.

"Hey Craig, It's Tom," I text. "My mom is in bed 17. As you can imagine I'm worried about her health and the general snags in the ED. I'm not sure what she's waiting on, is everything okay?"

Craig is the next doctor assigned to the area where my mom is being treated. I wrote and deleted a couple versions before sending that, trying to find a tone that was professional and direct but not overbearing. I really wanted to text in all caps, "TAKE BETTER CARE OF MY MOM!!" but that wouldn't solve anything.

Twenty minutes elapse without a response. So I call the ED and get a doctor on the line.

"Hey. It's Tom Fisher," I say in the friendliest tone I can muster.

"Hey there, what's up," Rebecca replies.

"My mom is in Room 17. I'm worried about her. I'd love to touch base with the doc."

My colleague walks the phone to the area near 17, and I overhear her say, "It's Tom. His mom is in 17. Who's in charge?" I hear shuffling, and Craig jumps on.

"I was just going to text. I was gathering info before I got back to you."

This breaks my tension. At the beginning of every shift Craig takes time to figure out what's going on with his patients. He's good with details and cares about people.

"The CT doesn't show anything worrisome. She might have a urinary tract infection."

"Cool. Thanks for the update. Hey, she let me know that she's in a lot of pain. Can you check on her?"

"Absolutely."

I don't really need to know what's been done. I can't process her data rationally anyway. I just want her to get back to ruthlessly mocking the Chicago Bears, listening to Mahler, and holding us all together. I know my colleagues are exceptional people and talented doctors. And in my heart I believe in equal treatment for everyone, that everyone in that emergency room matters equally. But right now I need them to save my mom from the hospital machinery that ignores pain, drags its feet on pain medication, and makes life-threatening treatment errors. Keep its sharp, grinding parts away from her body. I want to demand or beg them to protect her, do whatever it takes. But I just text a prompt, a reminder, and thanks. I will not force anything. I do my best to stay hopeful, but I've seen what can happen.

Two hours later the sun is setting, and Mom texts, "Can I go home?"

My first thought is that this is a question for her doctor. Has anyone checked on her? Is her nurse updating her? This woman who spent thirty-plus years as a school social worker trying to liberate children is now stuck in Bed 17. I'm trapped too—between marching down there to raise hell and simply disappearing from humiliation. What good am I if I know the system and still can't ensure one of the most important people in the world gets good care?

"They told me things look ok, but I'm in so much pain. I just want to be in my own bed."

"Did they discharge you?"

"I think so."

"Cool, they'll get you your paperwork."

For many Black women, complaining rarely gets solutions. More often, it leads to sanctions. So Mom seldom criticizes. She always presents her best self in the hope that institutions will treat her well. Is that why nobody has addressed her pain? Are they so busy that they can't consider my mom? If she has normal vitals and a normal CT, maybe it's just low-quality care and inhumane treatment without being dangerous. She went to the hospital because she was in misery, and that was never addressed. I have to look in her eyes to understand what's going on. I'll let her rest tonight and tomorrow will check in on her in person.

When I wake up the next morning the election is still undecided. After coffee and a shower, I head over to my parents' house, anxious about what I'll find. Given my regular exposure to sick COVID patients, it's been months since I've been inside with my family. I did all I could to avoid accidentally exposing my parents to the plague, but today Mom faces a threat and I need to see her eyes and assess her pain. I'll wear a mask and so will she and we'll hope for the best.

A parking spot is hard to find. By the time I reach her house, it's late morning, and she's still in bed. This is a woman who effortlessly chases after her grandchild and uses her rowing machine for exercise every day. While she's happy to see me, she winces with deep breaths and cringes every time she moves. I touch her side and she leaps.

"Mom, what are you taking? You're in a lot of pain!" I cannot believe what I'm seeing.

"Tylenol. Oh, it's much better!" she whispers through a grimace. Her heavy eyes show she hasn't slept.

If this is better, what was it like before? I order Italian food for our lunch and prod for more information. When we all settle around the kitchen table, I learn she never got a prescription, was never given discharge papers, and doesn't remember her diagnosis at all.

She waited until she couldn't wait anymore and then got up and left. This is a depressingly familiar scenario. I've searched for patients before only to find their room empty, with their blood pressure cuff, gown, and beeping monitor left behind. Every shift, patients float away from the waiting room and treatment areas precipitously and quietly, like balloons into the wind, never to return. While our blocked beds and throttled access to specialists force patients into unending waits, their lives aren't put on hold while they're here—they still have work to do and children to pick up. I long to rewind to the moment before they left to offer relief or answers—to let them know they matter. The hospital put Mom through this same mechanism of delay and disregard that grinds and pounds patients. I couldn't protect her. Justifying my inability to help leads nowhere. I've been there long enough to know that I'm part of the ineptitude.

After lunch, my sister takes my niece Corinne upstairs for a nap. Still in the kitchen, Mom, Dad, and I discuss the election and the warm weather. Mom holds a strained posture to ease her rib pain. In 2008 none of us could believe a Black South Sider could end up in the White House, and now we're skeptical that the president will be displaced. Mom's frequent grimaces return the conversation to her health. Even if she puts on a pleasant face, there's something wrong.

"Well, I'm taking Tylenol. Maybe that will help, but I started coughing up blood." She drops her eyes with the weight of this revelation.

"What?!" I stammer. "When did this start? Never mind. We have to act. We have to get you back to the hospital!"

I'm dizzy with the realization that side pain and coughing up blood is not a urinary tract infection or kidney stone, this is . . . *cancer*. Just as it is almost every time my previously healthy patients suddenly start coughing up blood. We counsel them not to jump to the worst-case scenario, but time after time their chest CT reveals a mass.

Should we send her back to my hospital? They'll have the benefit of yesterday's labs and radiology, but they just missed something serious. Maybe they'll do better this time, or maybe there is too much at stake now to let them fail twice? She's not angry with the care she received, she's embarrassed. Dad thinks she should go to her own doctor's hospital. She debates the matter and finally decides to go with his suggestion. Despite the lancing chest pain and hemoptysis, she showers, gets changed, and puts on lipstick. Dad gets ready, gathers his charger and reading material. Now alone in my childhood home, my sister and niece asleep upstairs, I feel sixteen all over again. As I did decades ago, I'm facing enormous threats and an uncertain future. Then it was violence. Now it's COVID. In both cases I can't do much to protect myself except to hide. But now Mom is sick, and I can't do anything. I can only accept what comes, but I feel unprepared, as though I'm sunbathing on the beach while a hurricane looms.

A half hour later my dad texts that they've arrived in the ED. Soon my sister wakes up and ambles down from her nap with my niece on her hip.

"Where is everyone?"

I'm planted in a living room chair, focused on the shadows cast on the floor by the sun filtering in through the trees, hoping Mom has a doctor who will proceed carefully and listen closely.

"Dad took Mom back to the hospital."

"Huh?" Lilla's eyes widen, and she sits down in a chair across from me.

When I share that Mom is coughing up blood, she bursts into heavy sobs. Fat tears run down her face and onto her pregnant belly. My niece touches her face and prompts Lilla to gather herself.

"It's okay, Corinne. Mama is sad."

I get up and hug them both closely.

My fear and sadness don't turn into tears. When upset, I experience a ringing in my head that reminds me of the pins and needles in my arm when I've slept wrong. I miss the time before, when that sensation would be pushed aside by a cleansing cry. After witnessing so many people lose limbs and lives over so many years, I don't know if I can cry anymore. I just wait for the ringing pins and needles to subside. At work, it passes quickly, and I get back to my job. But this isn't the hospital. The pins and needles stream from my head and consume my body.

"Lilla, why are you crying?" I ask. Maybe talking will help us both.

She tells me she feels so stupid. "She's been coughing for a while. A colleague at work coughed up blood and it turned out to be cancer. Why didn't I make her do something about it? I knew something was wrong."

"We don't know what's wrong yet. She's seeing about it right now. Let's not jump to worst-case scenarios."

But that's exactly what I myself have done. I'm certain it's lung cancer. Mom has been coughing for months. Her doctor called it acid reflux, but now, given the blood and pain, I'm certain that it's serious. From what I've seen, lung cancer is miserable. Relentless pain and trouble breathing marked by glimmers of hope that are inevitably dashed by recurrences. It will be unbearable to watch my mother dwindle away.

"Let's get out of here. Let's go for a walk," I say. I'm antsy for a change of scenery.

We bundle Corinne lightly, put her in the stroller, and head to the Point. After a right on Hyde Park Boulevard and a left on 55th Street, we cross under Lake Shore Drive. When I was a kid that underpass was graffitied and smelled of urine. Now it's clean and brightly lit, with a single tag scrawled in green spray paint that reads, "Defund. They Can't be Reformed." Promontory Point is a park jutting out into Lake Michigan where we've picnicked and biked for forty years. The Point is full of people dressed—or underdressed—for the unseasonably warm day. I push the stroller as we walk around the paved path. A couple in T-shirts stroll past holding hands. A group of six students reads together in the grass. A woman in jogging shorts and her leashed dog lie in the sun. We walk and silently take in the people and the warmth. Each tree and rock is associated with a time before. I exchange nods with a gray-bearded older gentleman sitting on a bench listening to the Isleys on his Bluetooth speaker. Hammocks strung between trees bulge with unseen people, only their book-holding hands visible. Soon the hospital and illness recede, freeing us to reminisce about our times in this park. The evening we saw teens throb to a drum circle, the air skunky with cannabis. The morning, with the sun still hanging low in the sky, that I learned to skip stones across flat water. And the afternoon we were drenched by the chilly spray of an unexpected wave crashing ashore.

We are seated on a sun-dappled bench when Dad returns us to 2020 with a text update: "The chest x-ray shows atelectasis, in the area of her pain."

Atelectasis. This means that a portion of her lung has collapsed. This is consistent with the tumor that I now *know* is threatening her life.

"Are they doing a CT scan?" I reply.

"Yes, that's next."

I'm bracing myself. I know in a few hours there will be bad news. I take Corinne out of her stroller to run around while Lilla shares that her colleague's lung cancer led to chemo, and she wasted away over a few years. First she stopped coming to the office, lost her independence, then her dignity, and finally her life. The struggle between aggressive treatment and a reconciliation with fate provides scant peace. With Corinne giggling and the lake glistening, we're entertaining loss.

Now nine months into the plague, loss is familiar. I've forfeited routines, predictability, and pleasure. And I've lost a partner. FaceTime, text, and email allowed a slow, almost imperceptible fade to my long-distance relationship with Monroe. In the past I'd believed the myth that "when it's right, it's easy." I now know there is no such thing as "the one" and that any partnership will require patience and perseverance. This time I threw aside those false slogans for the hard work of pushing past our difficult times. Despite our best efforts, without physical contact, our fears and communication gaps undermined what we built and made it impossible to solve conflict. The actions necessary to demonstrate love were thwarted by closed borders, a virus, and doubt. At some point we couldn't make out the contours of our relationship anymore, and after struggling along, we finally lost our ability to manage disagreements and confirm our bonds. The collapse tore a hole in my evenings, when we used to spend hours on the phone or watch movies together. Even bigger was the breach in my future. Life beyond the pandemic will not include at least one person I had planned to be a part of my life. Will it be only one, though?

Without travel, a partner, or much physical contact, my days are austere. While once I set goals years in advance, now I have a hard time considering what will come next month. I exist in the moment more than I thought possible. When I'm in a patient's room I do not long to be elsewhere. I focus on the details in their stories, observe their hands, and notice their movements. Hoping for children of my own is replaced by playing with my niece in the park. After a day in the hospital, the heat of my shower as it beats COVID off my tired body and the coolness of my sheets are enough. I fuss over the color of my Sunday-morning pancakes and memorialize them in photos. There is no five-year plan to execute. All I can do is protect my family, take care of people in my community, and find awe in everyday experiences. In many ways I have more satisfaction and meaning than in any other period. Sitting on this sunny bench with my sister, I have clarity.

This moment is fine. Facing north on the Point, I can see a grassy knoll, a firepit, and then craggy rocks that lead to a cove. In the distance, downtown high-rises break up the horizon. Bike riders pedal past us, seagulls create formations over the water, and the scent of cannabis gives the air density. My niece points

and laughs at a kite flying. Her curly brown halo picks up the
sun and ushers away any lingering turmoil. The numb ringing
in my head has long subsided. While I fear for my mother, I
know she is reconciled with death. When her time comes, she
wants to be cremated and scattered in the lake right here off the
Point. I want her end to be distant, obscure, and pain-free, but
few of us have that kind of end. With cancer comes a long battle
in alliance with the sorts of hospitals that will be as concerned
with her insurance as they are with her suffering. These mature
and efficient organizations are hardened and immovable after
decades of repetition. But that's tomorrow. There will always be
suffering, and our bodies are temporary, but together we have
something transcendent. Today we've found peace. And soon
my father will text with news about exactly what kind of challenge lies ahead.

The sun has set, and we are back at our parents' house when
that information arrives. Dad's text is simple: "Lots of clots—
both lungs."

"Oh no! Cancer?" I reply.

"Cancer not mentioned."

"Did you ask?"

"No. Said pulmonary emboli. No COVID. They're going to
admit her. Hematology consultation."

"Life is so short. We can't waste any of it," I text, not knowing how to respond.

This is a life-threatening illness but not the scenario we've
dreaded. It's difficult to release the certainty I had about a worst-
case situation. I search his texts for a stray word, reading between the lines and reinterpreting gaps to infer they simply
haven't found the lung cancer yet. Lilla's smile forces me to let it

go. Not having my experience caring for those at crossroads, she's simply accepted this good news. The worst may come, but today we fight a pulmonary embolism.

Pulmonary emboli are one of the life threats we're not allowed to miss in the Emergency Department. COVID has made PEs more common as the virus causes the blood to clot in places it's not supposed to: in hearts, causing heart attacks; in brains, leading to strokes; and in legs, creating clots that break free and float through veins into the lungs, where they're called pulmonary emboli. I've treated a number of PEs lately, and last week someone with a PE died in my care.

It was an overnight shift that was so busy, we never really caught up. At sign-out I accepted a gentleman in his fifties from the prior shift. His name was Mr. Franklin. He had COVID and was admitted for an irregular heart rate, a kidney injury, and a low blood-oxygen level. He was very ill but was stable enough for us to focus our attention on other patients while he waited for his bed upstairs. We scrambled from room to room as sick patients piled in. One hour turned to three, and a resident named David, in blue scrubs and with a thicket of dark hair, pulled me aside to ask, "Does Mr. Franklin seem sick to you?" It was the first time that I'd given the patient attention all shift, and I honestly did not know how he was doing. Together we opened his chart, reviewed the data, went to his room, and discussed his case. A COVID-positive patient with renal failure, a fast irregular heartbeat, and now borderline blood pressure. The only conclusion could be that this man is very sick and should be sent to the ICU immediately.

"Let's call the ICU," I said, "and get him transferred to their service."

The ICU doctor who would receive Mr. Franklin had been a resident just a couple years earlier. He was measured, patient, and immediately picked up on Mr. Franklin's decline, now eight hours after first arriving in the ED. He took over care, allowing me to return my attention to new patients. It was a couple hours before Mr. Franklin's nurse, Jimmy, asked me about his low blood pressure.

"He's been down here ten hours, and he's not looking good, Doc. I paged the ICU team. They didn't call me back."

Mr. Franklin's heart rate picked up, and his breathing became more labored. David and I considered a pulmonary embolism as the cause of all his problems. Before we attempted a diagnostic CT, we called the special team charged with intervening in life-threating PEs. David rolled an ultrasound machine into Mr. Franklin's room to determine his heart function. Our entire focus was now in Room 45.

"Oh, shit. He's got a clot in transit. Check this out." David was intently focused on the black-and-white ultrasound screen, where various shades of gray outline anatomy. Fluid is dark, solids are light, and our internal organs are a combination of the two, with patterns that delineate structure by the way they interface. David presented a ten-second loop of our patient's dark right ventricle, and in the middle there was a fluttering light gray blob. It was a blood clot in his heart. This is almost always fatal. A clot that size will inevitably float into his pulmonary artery and strain his heart to the point of failure. I asked Jimmy to prepare thrombolytics—we could not wait on the PE team or the ICU. As soon as I finished my words, Mr. Franklin stared off and the monitor struck a shrill alarm. Sitting upright, mouth agape, with one leg over the side of the bed, Mr. Franklin had stopped breathing.

I started moving reflexively: "Call a code, push epi, grab the cart, prep airway tools. . . ." And with that a team gathered, and a practiced choreography commenced. The pharmacist passed a nurse one milligram of epinephrine, and she pushed through an IV in his right arm. David moved smoothly and quickly. He set up his tools and effortlessly established an airway. A tech jumped on a stool and pumped Mr. Franklin's chest furiously. I asked a nurse to give the thrombolytic, and she launched it through that same IV. While our service was erratic when he was alive, now we were giving him everything we had as quickly as possible. Tech after tech pumped medications through his body with chest compressions until they were tired and sweaty.

Mr. Franklin had been awake and talking a couple hours ear-lier. Now, forty-five minutes into a resuscitation, his lids hung midway between open and closed, his eyes fixed on the unseen in a familiar death stare. Unable to find his pulse, we ended our efforts. After asking if anyone objected or had any ideas, I marked his death.

"Time of death at 5:32 A.M."

It was early in the morning, and we were exhausted. Silently we broke our PPE, washed our hands, and left the room. The ICU and PE intervention teams hovered outside the room, avoiding our eye contact.

"This always happens! They never take care of our sickest patients. This is the second PE who's died in the ER. I'm sick of it," David vented, his red, wet eyes flashing a fury that was otherwise cloaked by his mask and head cover.

It's hard to argue that we did the best we could for him. Mr. Franklin might have died anyway, but his cardiac arrest didn't have to happen in the ED. It had been ten hours since he entered the hospital. Why wasn't he in the ICU? Why didn't we diagnose a pulmonary embolism earlier? When I recount this death to my friends, they tell me I am not to blame. But if I know that the system is broken, isn't it my job to do more than avoid blame? Aren't I required to navigate the obstacles that block and delay care? If I simply let the system work, too many people will be hurt. If it's not my fault, whose fault is it?

My mom's health has been threatened by the same snafus. She now faces a less serious presentation of the same illness. She's in a hospital bed across town in a wealthier neighborhood. She has a diagnosis, her vital signs remain stable, the pain in her chest has been addressed, and she's begun blood thinners. Lilla texts calming information to my worried older sister, Ayanna, in San Francisco, and we await more news. She puts on Beyoncé's *Homecoming,* and my sweet niece, who only gets to view screens on very special occasions, is quickly mesmerized by the music and dancing. With so much now settled, I hug my sister with a long, thankful embrace, put on my shoes, and head home.

In a year of death, my mom's illness has reiterated the fragility of our bodies. Our present and whatever illusory future we may have are contingent on these temporary, flesh-and-blood structures. Without health we cannot love fully or hope expansively. We can only endure until the end. Our health is everything. We were fortunate. Mom had the physical reserve to endure, we were savvy enough to navigate the system, and she

has insurance that allowed her to go to any hospital. We won—
this time.

A few weeks after my mother's hospitalization I wrote a letter to the leaders of my hospital.

To Whom It May Concern,

Friday, my mother had her one-week follow-up appointment
after a pulmonary embolism admission. She gave me permission to
share that after presenting to an ED across town she was diagnosed, anticoagulated, worked up for a provocation, and discharged
in about 24 hours. She's recovering nicely, with a normal echo and
twice-daily apixaban.

Unfortunately, this admission followed a bad experience in our
own Emergency Department.

Despite the kindness of her ED team, not only was her problem
missed but she suffered needlessly with untreated pain. She went
home still hurting, without a diagnosis or follow-up plan. My colleagues did the best that they could for my mom, but these good
people were helpless in our system.

For too long fractured processes have remained unresolved. Instead of long-term solutions, we've patched over organizational
troubles and relied on work-arounds to protect VIP patients. Unfortunately, my mom received no such shelter. What happened to her
is unacceptable.

I write this as a son. A son whose mother agonized and had to
go elsewhere for care. A son of the South Side who has seen too
many of my neighbors languish in our ED. And a son of the University of Chicago, who has presided over just these kinds of cases and
who is haunted by patients I couldn't help.

I seek a reckoning: A strategic orientation that ensures our ED patients consistently receive prompt, high-quality care and everyone's mother is protected from harm. When this wave of COVID-19 recedes, I hope we can discuss institutional initiatives that promise humane care to all. I hope my mother's anguish can stimulate change.

I'd like to be part of the solution. We can do better. We must do better.

Tom

I have no reason to believe that any of this can or will change. But I don't know what else to do but to keep trying.

15

Dear Mom,

I did all I could to protect you, but it wasn't enough. When you came home just as sick as when you went to the hospital, the wave of nausea made my eyes water. Years of training, a network of colleagues, and an understanding of how health care screws people amounted to a hill of dust when it came time to keep you safe. As you know, I love the hospital, but just as you taught me, it is no different than any institution, a reflection of America. On that day you were simply a Black woman on the South Side, treated as so many Black women on the South Side are handled—the ER was too crowded, your caregivers too distracted, your suffering abstract. The system worked exactly as designed, not because you don't matter specifically but because none of us matter enough. You know the whole reason I chose this path was to understand and solve the traps that hurt us, and when I needed to free you, I couldn't. Real solutions may never happen, but let me tell you what a resolution would require.

Remember my medical school graduation? That sunny June afternoon in 2001, family came from Detroit, Topeka, Boston, and New Jersey. Uncle Louis brought a sample of my grandfather's wine in a plastic Welch's grape juice bottle. Decades ago, on the outskirts of Kansas City, Kansas, Grandfather Fisher (long since deceased) made that wine with grapes he grew on the land he owned with Grandma. Uncle Louis decanted Communion-sized pours into flimsy plastic cups, passed them around, and toasted to how his father had struggled, left school in the eighth grade, lived through Jim Crow, and seen men land on the moon. He let us know that Granddad made wine to celebrate and shared how proud he would have been to see me in that outfit. When he asked me what I wanted to do with medicine, with libations in hand, I said that I wanted "to care for the poor and shape a more just health-care system." With that we toasted to the ancestors, then sipped this antique tonic that burned and coated my throat on the way down. Now after two decades of trying to fulfill that mission, I know there cannot be justice in health or health care until there is justice in society.

This tension was introduced while still a medical student. I think I told you about my first rotation, when I cared for a child who had been shot on a playground. She was nine years old, with parted braids that ended with color-coordinated barrettes. Her clothes had been cut from her and lay in a heap on the floor. A bullet hole the size of a dime in the center of her chest wept a trickle of blood across her ribs to the side of the bed. When her shifting and gasping stopped and the heart monitor sounded the alarm signifying no cardiac activity, the word *thoracotomy* was spoken aloud by the senior doctors in the room. I didn't know enough to be helpful, so I just stood near the wall and watched. The senior resident made an incision across the left side of her chest, below her breast, and down her rib cage. From a silver tray full of clattering tools, he placed an implement that spread her ribs. A blood clot the size of a loaf of bread and the consistency of Jell-O fell to the floor. It smelled like a cross between metal and the ocean. Two resident surgeons worked quickly with deliberate fingers at the direction of the attending. Soon the child's heart was in one of their hands and being massaged. The monotone alarm that meant no heart rhythm floated over the din of doctors and nurses. Her stare never changed, and after a long twenty minutes she was pronounced dead. Her left arm flopped to the side, fingers pointing at the blood clot–covered floor.

In this girl I saw Lilla, as a child. I imagined her laughing while playing video games, just as my own baby sister did while I schooled her at Mario Brothers. Weren't we supposed to hold hands and say some words? Where was the news media? Who would be held responsible? Would my pounding heart slow down? My resident gestured at me. It was time to move on to the next patient. We debriefed as a team but there was no mourning. I knew what had happened to that child was not a clinical conundrum. It was bigger than medicine. At the time I first told you that story, you asked whether I still wanted to be a doctor. A veil lifted that day, but I couldn't understand what I had seen.

Over the next twenty years it gradually came into focus. In that time, I diagnosed lung cancer in nonsmokers and held children together who had been splashed onto the concrete by car collisions—bad luck befalls people of all kinds. While health disasters seem to fall from the heavens like rain, there are patterns in that morass of calamity. I've yet to see a white child suffer the fate of that little girl, shot while playing in the park. Our society has penned Black Chicagoans into a trap of racial segregation. It accepts their tax dollars and then disconnects city services, closes schools, and eliminates mental health facilities. Pervasive scams like predatory mortgages and payday loans extract their wealth, and bias limits their access to legiti-mate capital, leaving few businesses, stores, or opportunities. Then when our police are violent, unaccountable, and impotent to solve crimes, people take matters in their own hands. Bullets of all kinds fly in every direction. And some of them find their way into the chests of little girls. That bullet wasn't really stray. It was the logic of this coun-try finding its target. The same equation that makes it unusual for my wealthy patients to have kidney failure in their twenties, the same construction that offers my wealthy patients pathways that remove the possibility of interminable waits in the ER. These mechanisms, in operation repeatedly, steal years from South Side Chicagoans through early death and disability.

Mom, in two decades of caring for people on days they wish never happened and will never forget, I've learned something else—*everything*, our ability to create, love, and imagine, is contingent on the health of our bodies. When our bodies inevitably falter, restoring physical abilities falls to my ancient and intimate profession. In those moments when people teeter on that razor's edge of life and death, people often shed their masks of status and ego, revealing that which is most human. On those occasions, some demonstrate a grace and clarity that feels timeless, a connection to something that is in all of us. Then, as doctor and patient, we connect through essential ex-pressions of our humanity—reciprocity, listening, and honesty that sums to a level of trust rarely shared between strangers. And then I touch people right where it hurts, sometimes cutting them open in order to help them. Health care connects the most intimate parts of both patients and physicians. And this kind of familiarity means com-ing to terms with the fact that our bodies are the biological platform on which every other part of life stands—every single thing we do, individually and collectively. Our healthy bodies allow us to connect to one another, and to the infinite. Caring for our bodies and caring for each other is the necessary precondition of life. In other words, health is a human right—the thing we owe each other.

In your time in the ED, nobody loved you enough to resolve your suffering. My colleagues apologized for your experience, and I accepted their apologies. I know they couldn't do better. Over the path of my career, I too have struggled to honor this sacred pact in a health-care system that is deeply unjust and dangerous. Despite high-minded mandates to serve everyone, our establishments find ways to reject, defer, deny, and bankrupt many of those who seek care. In the end, the length of our lives and quality of our existence are silently transferred from poor to rich and from Black to white. These strategies are so embedded that this collection of actors would not perform better if their roles were reversed and all of a sudden the poor and Black had control of these broken systems. I can't protect my patients, and when it matters most, I couldn't turn an organization toward justice when it was on the line—and I couldn't protect you, Mom.

This cannot stand. Addressing the torments that send people to me weary and sick requires that America rearrange its allegiance to systems that subvert our inherent human value and absorb our bodies as inputs to a production function. If we accept that health is a human right, we then have a duty to ensure everyone has similar opportunity to flourish and can obtain necessary prevention, maintenance, and cure. This principle means a great deal to our entire society, as that is where health is created: by all of us, for all of us. But for us health-care professionals and doctors—members of the sector charged with healing our bodies—it is our sacred responsibility to honor the foundational philosophy that high-quality health care must be guaranteed to everyone. We must liberate health care from structures that create winners and losers because when our most important endowment is at stake, nobody can be allowed to lose. You are worthy of essential health care, Mom, as are all my patients. Resources like emergency services, basic medications, and prenatal care are fundamental. They must be provided to all without barriers, untethered to income or neighborhood. These strategic necessities elevate everyone, extend lives, and reduce suffering. Health care must reflect a commitment to the incalculable value of our bodies, and this means drastic change.

This isn't a new idea, this is old. Ensuring all Americans equal access to health care has been framed in several ways, including "universal care" or "health care for all." Over the years this imperative has been devalued, oversimplified, vilified, and shut down by cynical debate. Now I avoid these terms so that I do not contribute to the old political snares. Each in its own way, our peer countries are committed to health-care systems that provide essential services to the entire population—moral solutions that do not rob and take, but rather give. We too need a new arrangement, one that ceases the resource transfer from those at the bottom of society to those at the top, one that dismantles the separate tiers of our health-care system, one that invests in public health alongside innovation and treats everyone with the humanity we deserve. There are a lot of approaches to accomplish this that include new comprehensive strategies, but no matter what we call it, without a radical overhaul of our system, I can't guarantee you'll get better care in the future.

As you know, I spent a lot of time in a suit trying to understand how to make those changes. I learned that it is unlikely that greed, segregation, caste, and the other conditions that create injustice and poor health will collapse anytime soon. Everyone's health would improve if we could reshape society toward the truth that everyone is equally human, but we cannot throw up our hands and simply wait until that radical awakening happens—lives are at stake. We can improve our systems today and chart a path toward a more just future by guiding existing organizations and building new ones with key principles in mind: center humanity at every juncture. Elevate moral leaders. Address justice with systemic solutions.

I stumbled onto these ideas after years of confronting professional crises. Remember in the Great Recession when the hospital handled financial headwinds by limiting care for the poor in order to provide for the rich? Then a few years later, I led a layoff in order to protect my company's balance sheet? While most workdays were normal, those calamitous situations where humanity and profit competed forced hard decisions and shaped health-care systems and lives—including my own. Each time we chose wrong, we entrenched inequity. These sorts of choices led to a system where your suffering would be dismissed and your diagnosis missed. All of this came from the same place: a merciful distribution of resources clashed with generating surplus, and time after time, profit won. This impulse is a pox on society, but in health care it is intolerable. You were hurt because we have optimized a system to profit at the expense of humanity, led by teams of managers who do not incorporate morality in their assessments.

A system that has been refined over generations is resistant to change. Executives, vendors, physicians, insurers, pharmaceutical companies, suppliers of medical technology—the entire medical-industrial complex grows fat as long as nothing changes. Our unequal system and the vast sums spent on health care represent these parties' income, and they will oppose reforms that would slow down the transfer of societal resources to their control. While we already have enough information and even good tactical plans, each of these solutions faces the ultimate paradox of U.S. health policies: the more likely a proposal is to deliver true equity, the less likely it is to be viable. Those of us who wish to do more, in a different way, have to win every battle, while the status quo only has to delay in order to derail progress. Individuals on the inside aren't enough against a hardened system; even a handful of teams driving for change within an institution are unlikely to be sufficient. A humane and just system requires everyone to come together—all of us as citizens—and demand moral transformation.

I love you, Mom, and I was unable to save you, and maybe nobody could. Over the course of almost twenty years of practice and experience, I have realized that there are a lot of ways to make things better once we recognize health care is a love story: my love for you, a community's love of that child shot on the playground, our society's love for the families that hold vigils outside the ER for their wounded young men. And as with all love, once we've committed, we will encounter difficulty and fail at times, but it is then, especially then, that we must continue to demonstrate our love through actions.

You fell into the same trap as my other patients. A snare as big and as old as the country itself. Fixing it and building a healthy population requires a revolution in the way we view humanity, clarity in the trade-offs we're making, and honesty about the costs embedded in seemingly neutral decisions. In the process we must face the damage we've accepted in the name of profit, elevate moral leadership, reconcile conflicting truths with honorable new systems—and protect the lives of my worthy and beautiful patients who seem doomed from the start. Only then can we follow steps toward better health and a better health-care system for America, one that is just and true.

Onward,

tlf

ACKNOWLEDGMENTS

Everything I have accomplished in life has resulted from the immense support of others. The ups and downs captured in this book, and the book itself, emerge from a community. I can never fully capture how my parents, Thomas and Julie, built a home full of love and encouragement. With their foundation of stability and safety I was able to flourish, to take risks and explore. They have continued to be a source of strength across the years. Thank you. My sisters, Ayanna and Lilla, filled my life with love and laughter from the beginning. I could not have survived and maintained my sanity through the madness of 2020 without the daily walks with Lilla and Corinne and the Sunday family picnics that included her husband, Chris. Thank you all.

I wrote this book mostly in the COVID pandemic of 2020. Thank you to so many people whose words of fellowship reminded me that I was part of something bigger and that this too shall pass. College friends never let me disappear into worry and fear. Thank you, Nada Llewellyn, Julian O'Connor, Joe Ybarra, Federico Rivera, and Ray Sosa. Eve Ewing and Damon Jones, thank you for plying me with baked goods and conversation, sweets that brightened my spirits. Jason Dempsey, thank you for teaching me courage and perseverance in the face of life-threatening odds; I would not have made it through without your insights. Thank you, Kaye Wilson, for checking in on me and for the years of fortification at your kitchen table. My brothers and sisters Maurice Smith, Natalie Moore, Mike Toca, Yancey Hrbowski, Sunny Ramshandani, Danita Harris, Kenyatta Matthews, and Felicia Cummings (Graves): as you had for decades before, you all held me down with daily words and laughs. You all reminded me that my patients need my head in the game and my words on the page. Lastly, thanks to Free The Land Collective; our game nights brightened my evenings with jokes and love. And peace to Jamaica Drip; our music and sports commentary gave me a source of grounding and normalcy.

A midwife to the birth of this book is the Aspen Health Innovators Fellowship. Those two years immersed in a community of openness and honesty gave me the courage to look closely at what I've learned and follow what I'm meant to do. In particular, thanks to The Justice League and my small group of Evan Melrose and Chris Brandt.

The University of Chicago section of emergency medicine has been my clinical home for twenty years. I have trained and been trained by decades of doctors and nurses. Through ups and downs, you all (doctors, nurses, techs, RTs, pharmacists, registration, security, and EVS) serve society in moments that are unimaginable to most, and you do it with courage and humanity. Without your guidance and inspiration, I am not here. Thank you for counting me among your ranks.

Thank you to Adam Serwer and Jelani Cobb for listening to my perspective over the years and pointing out that I need to write. Thanks to Ta-Nehisi Coates for ignoring my belief that "I am a doctor, not a writer," mentoring my writing process, and decoding what writing means. This book only happens with our decades of friendship and conversation.

A few folks have read early versions and provided early ideas to make this book better. Thank you, Dawnie Walton, Ben Talton, and Raegan McDonald-Mosley.

Thanks to Gloria Loomis for taking on this project and shepherding it along. And thank you to Chris Jackson. One day we were in conversation and you said something like, "Come on, let's do a book." Thank you for your patience while I learned how, for taking my world seriously, and for your prodigious genius that led to this product.

Onward,

tlf

NOTES

3. Dear Janet

37 **Between 1916 and 1970:** "Great Migration," *Encyclopedia of Chicago,* accessed August 11, 2021, encyclopedia.chicagohistory.org/pages/545.html.

38 ***Dorothy Gautreaux et al. v. Chicago Housing Authority:*** "The Gautreaux Lawsuit," Business and Professional People for the Public Interest, accessed August 29, 2021, bpichicago.org/programs/housing-community-development/public-housing/gautreaux-lawsuit/.

38 **Seven hundred thousand jobs:** Alana Semuels, "Chicago's Awful Divide," *The Atlantic,* March 28, 2018, theatlantic.com/business/archive/2018/03/chicago-segregation-poverty/556649/.

39 **less than half of the local minimum wage:** Semuels, "Chicago's Awful Divide."

39 **almost 80 percent of the population:** Marynia Kolak, Daniel Block, and Myles Wolf, "Food Deserts Persist in Chicago Despite More Supermarkets," *The Chicago Reporter,* October 3, 2018.

43 **942 people murdered:** "Homicides in Chicago, 1965–1995

(ICPSR 6399)," Institute for Social Research, University of Michigan, accessed August 11, 2021, icpsr.umich.edu/web/NACJD/studies/6399.

5. Dear Nicole

73 **Eight doctors in Michigan:** "About ACEP," American College of Emergency Physicians, accessed August 11, 2021, acep.org/who-we-are/about-us/.

74 **over a span of thirteen dense pages:** "Emergency Department Planning and Resource Guidelines," American College of Emergency Physicians, accessed August 11, 2021, acep.org/globalassets/new-pdfs/policy-statements/emergency-department-planning-and-resource-guidelines.pdf.

76 **analyzed 140 million visits:** "National Hospital Ambulatory Medical Care Survey: 2017 Emergency Department Summary Tables," Centers for Disease Control and Prevention, accessed August 11, 2021, cdc.gov/nchs/data/nhamcs/web_tables/2017_ed_web_tables-508.pdf.

78 **bias in the algorithm:** Casey Ross, " 'Nobody Is Catching It': Algorithms Used in Health Care Nationwide Are Rife with Bias," *STAT,* June 21, 2021, statnews.com/2021/06/21/algorithm-bias-playbook-hospitals/.

79 **47 percent reported being physically assaulted:** "ACEP Emergency Department Violence Poll Research Results," American College of Emergency Physicians, accessed August 11, 2021, emergencyphysicians.org/globalassets/files/pdfs/2018acep-emergency-department-violence-pollresults-2.pdf.

80 **Emergency Medical Treatment and Active Labor Act:** "Emergency Medical Treatment & Labor Act (EMTALA)," Centers for Medicare and Medicaid Services, accessed August 11, 2021, cms.gov/Regulations-and-Guidance/Legislation/EMTALA.

81 **otherwise be available to serve:** Clayton Dalton and Daniel Tonellato, "Opinion: Emergency Rooms Shouldn't Be Parking Lots for Patients," National Public Radio, November 30, 2019,

npr.org/sections/health-shots/2019/11/30/783278033/opinion
-emergency-rooms-shouldnt-be-parking-lots-for-patients?ft
=nprml&f=1001.

82   **According to a 2012 study:** Benjamin C. Sun et al., "Effect of
      Emergency Department Crowding on Outcomes of Admitted
      Patients," *Annals of Emergency Medicine* 61, no. 6 (December
      2012): 605–11, doi.org/10.1016/j.annemergmed.2012.10.026.

82   **health-care equivalent of a rolling blackout:** Arthur Keller-
      mann, "Crisis in the Emergency Department," *New England Jour-
      nal of Medicine* 355, no. 13 (October 2006): 1300–1303, doi.org/
      10.1056/NEJMp068194.

7. Dear Robert

103   **an aspirational definition of health:** "Constitution," World
      Health Organization, accessed August 12, 2021, who.int/about/
      governance/constitution.

105   **Insulin's role in diabetes was discovered:** "The Nobel Prize in
      Physiology or Medicine 1923," The Nobel Prize, accessed
      August 12, 2021, nobelprize.org/prizes/medicine/1923/summary/.

106   **5 to 10 percent of your overall health:** "Determinants of
      Health," *GoInvo,* accessed August 12, 2021, goinvo.com/vision/
      determinants-of-health/.

106   **almost 10 percent of Americans lived in food deserts:** Christi-
      anna Silva, "Food Insecurity in the U.S. by the Numbers," Na-
      tional Public Radio, September 27, 2020, npr.org/2020/09/27/
      912486921/food-insecurity-in-the-u-s-by-the-numbers.

106   **almost 80 percent of the people:** Kevin Quinn, "Food Deserts
      in Chicago," *Story Maps,* April 10, 2020, storymaps.arcgis.com/
      stories/e22a3369845340cf8a62d3e0d20a5f0b.

107   **30 to 40 percent to our physical and mental well-being:** "De-
      terminants."

107   **34 percent of adults do not get regular:** "Adult Physical In-
      activity," *Chicago Health Atlas,* accessed August 12, 2021,

chicagohealthatlas.org/indicators/HCSPA?topic=adult-physical
-inactivity.

107   **but 30 percent smoke:** "Adult Smoking Rate," *Chicago Health
      Atlas,* accessed August 12, 2021, chicagohealthatlas.org/
      indicators/HCSSMKP?topic=adult-smoking-rate.

107   **contributes 20 to 30 percent to your health status:** "Determi-
      nants."

108   **25 percent are unemployed:** "Unemployment Rate," *Chicago
      Health Atlas,* accessed August 12, 2021, chicagohealthatlas.org/
      indicators/UMP?topic=unemployment-rate.

108   **23 percent do not graduate from high school:** "High School
      Graduation Rate," *Chicago Health Atlas,* accessed August 12, 2021,
      chicagohealthatlas.org/indicators/EDB?topic=high-school
      -graduation-rate.

108   **a life expectancy of fifty-nine years:** Kristen Thometz, "Chi-
      cago Has the Largest Life Expectancy Gap in the Country.
      Why?" *WTTW,* June 6, 2019, news.wttw.com/2019/06/06/
      chicago-has-largest-life-expectancy-gap-country-why.

109   **20 percent of your health:** "Determinants."

110   **male-female partners who are related by a social bond:** J. Gra-
      ham Ruby et al., "Estimates of the Heritability of Human Lon-
      gevity Are Substantially Inflated Due to Assortative Mating,"
      Genetics 210, no. 3 (November 2018): 1109–24, doi.org/10.1534/
      genetics.118.301613.

110   **In 1930 the U.S. Census counted:** "1930," United States Census
      Bureau, accessed August 12, 2021, census.gov/history/www/
      through_the_decades/index_of_questions/1930_1.html.

110   **more likely to live close to their parents:** Quoctrung Bui and
      Claire Cain Miller, "The Typical American Lives Only 18 Miles
      from Mom," *The New York Times,* December 23, 2015, nytimes.
      com/interactive/2015/12/24/upshot/24up-family.html.

111   **Black Americans owned 0.5 percent of the national wealth:**
      Calvin Schermerhorn, "Why the Racial Wealth Gap Persists,

More Than 150 Years After Emancipation," *The Washington Post,*
June 19, 2019, washingtonpost.com/outlook/2019/06/19/why
-racial-wealth-gap-persists-more-than-years-after-emancipation/.

9. Dear Dania

135   **more than twenty million American workers:** Earlene Dowell,
"Census Bureau's 2018 County Business Patterns Provides Data
on Over 1,200 Industries," United States Census Bureau, October
14, 2020, census.gov/library/stories/2020/10/health-care-still
-largest-united-states-employer.html.

135   **we spent \$1.2 trillion on hospitals:** "Health Expenditures,"
Centers for Disease Control and Prevention, accessed August 12,
2021, cdc.gov/nchs/fastats/health-expenditures.htm.

135   **each American spending \$11,172 per person:** "Health Expendi-
tures," Centers for Disease Control and Prevention.

136   **A visit to the ER averages:** Ken Alltucker, " 'Really Astonish-
ing': Average Cost of Hospital ER Visit Surges 176% in a Decade,
Report Says," *USA Today,* June 4, 2019, usatoday.com/story/
news/health/2019/06/04/hospital-billing-code-changes-help
-explain-176-surge-er-costs/1336321001/.

136   **in the ICU is about \$4,000:** Catherine Tak Piech, "Daily Cost of
an Intensive Care Unit Day: The Contribution of Mechanical
Ventilation," *Critical Care Medicine* 33, no. 6 (July 2005): 1266–71,
researchgate.net/journal/Critical-Care-Medicine-0090-3493.

136   **the average stay in the hospital for COVID-19:** Hillary Hof-
fower, "If You're Hospitalized with COVID-19 and Don't Have
Insurance, You'll Likely Owe \$73,000. One Chart Shows How
Broken the System Is for the Most Vulnerable," *Business Insider,*
March 27, 2020, businessinsider.com/coronavirus-covid-19
-treatment-testing-costs-2020-3?op=1.

136   **about \$475,000 for a course:** Tony Hagen, "Novartis Sets a Price
of \$475,000 for CAR T-Cell Therapy," *OncLive,* August 30, 2017,
onclive.com/view/novartis-sets-a-price-of-475000-for-car-tcell
-therapy.

136 **a dose of remdesivir:** Catherine Thorbecke, "Coronavirus Drug Remdesivir to Cost $3,120 per Patient with Private Insurance, Irking Critics," ABC News, June 29, 2020, abcnews.go .com/US/covid-19-drug-remdesivir-cost-3120-us-patients/ story?id=71509977.

137 **employers responded by offering:** Thomas Buchmueller and Alan Monheit, "Employer-Sponsored Health Insurance and the Promise of Health Insurance Reform," *Inquiry* 46 (Summer 2009): 187–202, journals.sagepub.com/doi/pdf/10.5034/ inquiryjrnl_46.02.187.

137 **they covered about 160 million:** "Health Insurance Coverage of the Total Population," Kaiser Family Foundation, accessed August 12, 2021, kff.org/other/state-indicator/total-population/.

138 **protected around 61 million people:** "An Overview of Medicare," Kaiser Family Foundation, accessed August 12, 2021, kff.org/other/state-indicator/total-population/.

138 **covers about 75 million low-income adults and children:** Robin Rudowitz, Rachel Garfield, and Elizabeth Hinton, "10 Things to Know about Medicaid: Setting the Facts Straight," Kaiser Family Foundation, March 6, 2019, kff.org/medicaid/ issue-brief/10-things-to-know-about-medicaid-setting-the-facts -straight/.

138 **reaches about 6 million people:** "Children's Health Insurance Program (CHIP)," Medicaid, accessed August 12, 2021, medicaid .gov/chip/index.html.

139 **Medicare drove the racial integration:** Janell Ross, "The Massive Role that Medicare Played in Racial Integration," *The Washington Post,* July 31, 2015, washingtonpost.com/news/the-fix/ wp/2015/07/31/the-massive-role-that-medicare-played-in-racial -integration/.

139 **Given this market power:** Eric Lopez, Tricia Neuman, Gretchen Jacobson, and Larry Levitt, "How Much More Than Medicare Do Private Insurers Pay? A Review of the Literature," Kaiser Family Foundation, April 15, 2020, kff.org/medicare/

issue-brief/how-much-more-than-medicare-do-private-insurers
-pay-a-review-of-the-literature/.

139 **more than 27 percent of the Illinois budget:** "Interactive Budget," State of Illinois, accessed August 12, 2021, www2.illinois
.gov/sites/budget/Pages/InteractiveBudget.aspx.

140 **Illinois Medicaid pays 61 cents:** "Medicaid-to-Medicare Fee
Index," Kaiser Family Foundation, accessed August 12, 2021, kff
.org/medicaid/state-indicator/medicaid-to-medicare-fee-index/.

140 **Seven in ten of the 28 million uninsured:** Jennifer Tolbert,
Kendal Orgera, and Anthony Damico, "Key Facts about the Uninsured Population," Kaiser Family Foundation, November 6,
2020, kff.org/uninsured/issue-brief/key-facts-about-the
-uninsured-population/.

140 **generally less than 2 percent of total revenue:** Alex Kacik,
"Top Not-for-Profit Hospitals Offer Disproportionately Less
Charity Care, Study Finds," *Modern Healthcare,* February 18, 2021,
modernhealthcare.com/providers/top-not-profit-hospitals-offer
-disproportionately-less-charity-care-study-finds.

141 **difficult for your patients to stay healthy if they're uninsured:**
"Key Facts," Kaiser Family Foundation.

141 **one in five uninsured adults:** "Key Facts," Kaiser Family Foundation.

141 **less likely than those with insurance:** "Key Facts," Kaiser Family Foundation.

141 **more likely to be hospitalized for avoidable health problems:**
"Key Facts," Kaiser Family Foundation.

141 **uninsured people receive fewer diagnostic:** "Key Facts," Kaiser
Family Foundation.

141 **are 50 percent more likely than white people:** "Key Facts,"
Kaiser Family Foundation.

141 **in nearby Englewood 12.3 percent are uninsured:** "Uninsured
Rate," *Chicago Health Atlas,* accessed August 13, 2021,
chicagohealthatlas.org/indicators/UNS?topic=uninsured-rate.

141   **doctors and hospitals concentrated on the whiter North Side:**
      Juliet Yonek and Romana Hasnain-Wynia, "A Profile of Health
      and Health Resources Within Chicago's 77 Community Areas,"
      Center for Healthcare Equity/Institute for Healthcare Studies,
      Feinberg School of Medicine, Northwestern University, 2011,
      news.wttw.com/sites/default/files/Chicago-Health-Resources
      -Report-2011-0811.pdf.

143   **twice as much funding as the hospitals with the lowest share:**
      Karyn Schwartz and Anthony Damico, "Distribution of CARES
      Act Funding Among Hospitals," Kaiser Family Foundation,
      May 13, 2020, kff.org/health-costs/issue-brief/distribution-of
      -cares-act-funding-among-hospitals/.

143   **privately insured patients got twice the relief:** Jesse Drucker,
      Jessica Silver-Greenberg, and Sarah Kliff, "Wealthiest Hospitals
      Got Billions in Bailout for Struggling Health Providers," *The
      New York Times,* May 25, 2020, nytimes.com/2020/05/25/
      business/coronavirus-hospitals-bailout.html.

144   **had to wait weeks before landing economic relief:** Paige Win-
      field Cunningham, "The Health 202: Medicaid Providers Had to
      Wait Weeks for Coronavirus Relief Dollars," *The Washington
      Post,* June 12, 2021, washingtonpost.com/news/powerpost/
      paloma/the-health-202/2020/06/12/the-health-202-medicaid
      -providers-had-to-wait-weeks-for-coronavirus-relief-dollars/
      5ee255c188e0fa32f82388f9/.

11. Dear Richard

164   **"I'd rather go home":** David Beiser, Notes, February 12, 2009.

165   **In a medical journal:** Laurence D. Hill and James L. Madara,
      "Role of the Urban Academic Medical Center in US Health
      Care," *Journal of the American Medical Association* 294, no. 17 (No-
      vember 2005): 2219–20, doi:10.1001/jama.294.17.2219.

167   **The *Chicago Tribune* wrote:** Jason Grotto, "Mauled by Dog, Kid
      Sent Home by ER," *Chicago Tribune,* February 13, 2009,

chicagotribune.com/news/ct-xpm-2009-02-13-0902130117-story
.html.

12. September 2020

181   **made up 72 percent of the deaths:** Natalie Moore, "In Chicago,
      COVID-19 Is Hitting the Black Community Hard," National
      Public Radio, April 6, 2020, npr.org/sections/coronavirus-live
      -updates/2020/04/06/828303894/in-chicago-covid-19-is-hitting
      -the-black-community-hard.

181   **a fifth of those who died:** Karen Yourish, K. K. Rebecca Lai,
      Danielle Ivory, and Mitch Smith, "One-Third of All U.S. Corona-
      virus Deaths Are Nursing Home Residents or Workers," *The
      New York Times,* May 11, 2020, nytimes.com/interactive/2020/
      05/09/us/coronavirus-cases-nursing-homes-us.html.

181   **121 residents fell ill:** Robert Gebeloff et al., "The Striking Racial
      Divide in How Covid-19 Has Hit Nursing Homes," *The New York
      Times,* May 21, 2020, nytimes.com/2020/05/21/us/coronavirus
      -nursing-homes-racial-disparity.html.

181   **an astronomical infection rate:** Cheryl Corley, "The COVID-19
      Struggle in Chicago's Cook County Jail," National Public Radio,
      April 13, 2020, npr.org/2020/04/13/833440047/the-covid-19
      -struggle-in-chicagos-cook-county-jail.

181   **the incarcerated and the incarcerators:** Bill Hutchinson,
      "COVID-19 Outbreak at Virginia Jail Infects 124 Inmates, 20 Staff-
      ers: Officials," ABC News, September 10, 2020, abcnews.go
      .com/US/covid-19-outbreak-virginia-jail-infects-124-inmates/
      story?id=72925115; Rick Sobey, "Coronavirus Outbreak at Massa-
      chusetts Jail Expands, Up to 48 Cases Reported," *Boston Herald,*
      October 4, 2020, bostonherald.com/2020/10/04/coronavirus
      -outbreak-at-massachusetts-jail-expands-up-to-48-cases-reported/.

182   **homicide rates fell:** Thomas Abt, Richard Rosenfeld, and Er-
      nesto Lopez, "COVID-19 and Homicide: Final Report to Arnold
      Ventures," accessed 13 August 2021, craftmediabucket.s3

.amazonaws.com/uploads/COVID-19-Homicide_061520
_Final.pdf.

183   **And then Chicago exploded:** Neil MacFarquhar and Robert
      Chiarito, "Chicago Gun Violence Spikes and Increasingly Finds
      the Youngest Victims," *The New York Times,* July 5, 2020, nytimes
      .com/2020/07/05/us/chicago-shootings.html.

183   **house just 1.5 percent of the population:** German Lopez,
      "How to Dramatically Reduce Gun Violence in American Cit-
      ies," *Vox,* July 12, 2019, vox.com/policy-and-politics/2019/7/12/
      20679091/thomas-abt-bleeding-out-urban-gun-violence-book
      -review.

INDEX

ABOUT THE AUTHOR

THOMAS FISHER is a board-certified emergency medicine physician from Chicago. He has worked to improve health care as an academic, health insurance executive, and White House Fellow in the first term of the Obama administration. His path includes training in the Robert Wood Johnson Clinical Scholars Program, being honored as one of *Crain's Chicago Business's* 40 Under 40, and inclusion in the Aspen Institute's Health Innovators Fellowship. He is an epicure and a runner, and for the past twenty years he has worked in the emergency department at the University of Chicago, serving the same South Side community where he was raised.

Twitter: @tfishermd